Working with the English Anthology

John Seely
David Kitchen
Clare Constant

Heinemann Educational Publishers
Halley Court, Jordan Hill, Oxford OX2 8EJ
A division of Reed Educational and Professional Publishing Ltd

MELBOURNE AUCKLAND FLORENCE
PRAGUE MADRID ATHENS
SINGAPORE TOKYO SÃO PAULO
CHICAGO PORTSMOUTH (NH) MEXICO
IBADAN GABORONE JOHANNESBURG
KAMPALA NAIROBI

First published 1996

2000 99 98
10 9 8

ISBN 0 435 10186 2

Designed and typeset by **AMR**
Cover illustration by Martin Jones
Printed and bound in the UK by Bath Press

Acknowledgements
The Authors and Publishers should like to thank the following for permission to use photographs/copyright material:
Carcanet Press Ltd for 'Wil Williams' by Gillian Clarke from *Letting in the Rumour*, p24; 'Jac Codi Baw' by Gillian Clarke from *Selected Poems* 1985, p26; 'No Hands' by Gillian Clarke from *The King of Britain's Daughter* 1993, p28; 'Sunday' by Gillian Clarke p30 and 'The Field-Mouse' p32 by Gillian Clarke from *Letter from a Far Country* 1982; Faber & Faber Ltd for 'The Early Purges' by Seamus Heaney from *Seven Modern Poets – 1974*, p39; 'Follower' by Seamus Heaney p43, 'Digging' p44 and 'Mid-Term Break' p47 by Seamus Heaney from *Death of a Naturalist – New Selected Poems 1990*; 'Storm on the Island' by Seamus Heaney from *Death of a Naturalist – 1966 and 1991*, p49; Nissim Ezekiel for 'Night of the Scorpion' from *Latter Day Psalms* Oxford University Press India, p54; Alice Walker for 'Poem at Thirty-Nine' from *Horses make a Landscape more Beautiful* The Women's Press, p57; © Chinua Achebe for 'Vultures' from *Beware Soul Brother* Heinemann Educational Books, p60; Taufiq Rafat for 'Sacrifice' from *Pieces of Eight. Eight Poets from Pakistan* edited by Yunis Said, Oxford University Press Pakistan 1971, p62; Anne Wilkinson © Alan G. Wilkinson for 'A Cautionary Tale', Macmillan Canada, p64; Nissim Ezekiel for 'Poverty Poems – 2' from *Collected Poems* Oxford University Press India, p69; The Bodley Head for extract from 'Mama Dot' from *Mama Dot* by Fred D'Aguiar, p71; © Edward Kamau Brathwaite for 'Limbo' from *The Arrivants* by permission of Oxford University Press 1973, p72; Bogle l'Ouverture Publications for 'Wha Fe Call I' by Valerie Bloom from *Touch mi! Tell mi!* p75; © Pierre Coupey for 'Study No. X' from *Bring Forth The Cowards*, McGill Poetry Series 1964, p78; Grace Nichols for 'For Forest' from *Lazy Thoughts of a Lazy Woman* Virago Press 1989, p81.

The Publishers have made every effort to trace the copyright holders, but if they have inadvertently overlooked any, they will be pleased to make the necessary arrangements at the first opportunity.

The Publishers should like to thank the following for permission to reproduce photographs on the pages noted.

Yale Centre for British Art, Paul Mellon Collection, p5; by kind permission of The Provost and Fellows of Kings College Cambridge, p6; John Wells/Science Photo Library, p8; Nils Jorgensen/Rex Features, p10; Neil Libbert/Network, p11; Gideon Mendel/Network, p13; by kind permission of The Provost and Fellows of Kings College Cambridge, p15; Arnulf Husmo/© Tony Stone Images, Rod Williams/Bruce Coleman Ltd, p16; courtesy Carcanet Press, p21; © Milepost, Christopher Hill Photographic, p24; © Chris Walsh/Britstock IFA, p26; courtesy RAF, p28; John Seely, p30; © Maurice Walker, p32; © Caroline Forbes, p37; © Arthur Christiansen/Frank Lane Picture Agency, p39; © S & O Mathews, p43; Barnaby's Picture Library,p 44; Geoffrey Schofield/Barnaby's Picture Library, p47; Frank Lane Picture Agency, p49; Christian Aid/Achinto, p54; Sally & Richard Greenhill, p57; © Britstock IFA/Aberham, p60; © Britstock IFA/Roger Cracknell, p64; Börge Tobiasson/Panos Pictures, p67; Centrepoint, p69; © Fotomas Index, p71; Les Barry/Barnaby's Picture Library, p72; Nicola Sutton, p75; Bruce Coleman Limited, p81; Heinemann International, p88; © Ronen Numa, p90; courtesy of the Women's Press, p91.

Contents

Introduction

An examination is not an ideal occasion to have to think and write about poetry. If you are a lover of poetry it probably seems a very false idea – to be examined on how well you can express your thoughts and feelings about something that has possibly had a big impact on you. And if poetry is not your favourite reading, then being assessed on it isn't likely to make you want to read more. But ...

Everyone who enters for GCSE English has to write about poetry, and for many this will take the form of being examined on the *NEAB Anthology*. We have prepared this book not just to make taking the exam less daunting – although we certainly hope it will – but to help you read the poems as poems and to enjoy and learn from the experience.

This book contains the full text* of all the poems set in the *NEAB Anthology* for English. We have added stimulating photographs; not only to make the book more appealing, but also to help create the right atmosphere to read and appreciate the poems. We have also provided background information about the writers. In the section called *The poets*, this comes in the introduction to each poet, and in *Poems from other cultures and traditions* this information comes in an alphabetical dictionary starting on page 88.

We have arranged the poems differently, too. We have kept the main sections, but within them we have put the poems in the best order for people reading them for the first time; for example it is possible to work your way through the section on Seamus Heaney, stage by stage. As you read and think about each poem you will be developing insights and skills that you can use when you come to the next poem.

In the section called *Poems from other cultures and traditions* we have grouped the poems together by theme so that you can read two or three poems that have similar subject matter or that follow similar patterns. Since the examiners often ask questions about themes in the poems, this should prove helpful.

Each section has advice and practice for the examination. In addition there is a short section in the *Conclusion* which gives advice on preparing for the examination and writing good answers. There is also a *Glossary* – a list of technical terms you can use when speaking or writing about poetry. The practice questions for the examination and the content of *Working with the English Anthology* have been discussed with NEAB senior examiners.

* The correct versions of 'The Human Abstract', 'Vultures' and 'Limbo' are as they appear in this book. Where necessary, you will have been given amendments to the *Anthology* by the NEAB.

1 William Blake

—— His life ——

William Blake was born in London in 1757. From an early age he was interested in drawing and when he was ten he went to a drawing school. From here, when he was fifteen he became an apprentice to an engraver, James Basire. Later he went to the recently founded Royal Academy, so although he started writing poetry at an early age, all his education was in drawing and engraving. When he was 22, he got a job as an engraver to a bookseller and publisher. Three years later he married Catherine Boucher.

Blake continued to write and his first book of poems was published in 1783. The next year, when he was 27, he set up his own business as an engraver. From then on, while he earned his living making engravings, he expressed his vision of the world through writing and illustrating poetry. His first major work to be produced in this way was *Songs of Innocence*, which he produced in 1789. It was followed five years later by *Songs of Experience*. All the poems in this selection are taken from *Songs of Innocence and of Experience*.

— Blake the artist-craftsman —

Blake produced his books entirely with his own skills. He wrote the poems, drew the illustrations and designed the pages himself. Then he engraved the plates from which they were produced. After he had printed the pages, he coloured them by hand. This is what one of his most famous poems, 'London', looked like in the original version of *Songs of Experience*.

—— Blake's picture —— of the world

William Blake grew up in a time of enormous and rapid change. In France the old government of King and aristocrats was swept away in a bloody revolution. In Britain the industrial and agricultural revolutions changed people's lives for ever. At the beginning of the eighteenth century most people lived in the countryside and earned their living from farming; a hundred years later the majority of men and women lived in towns and worked in factories. Towns and cities grew rapidly and conditions were often dirty, diseased and dangerous. Even the landscape changed. The old open countryside was fenced off into the patchwork of enclosed fields that we still see today; the old freedom to roam across open fields had gone for ever.

Blake was deeply aware of the effects that these changes were having on people's lives. He saw men and women becoming less free and more oppressed by the powerful economic forces that were at work. But he was also sensitive to the ways in which this changed their moral and emotional lives. He did not separate politics, religion and the imagination; they were all parts of the same world.

—— Key images ——

Blake wrote a huge amount, but throughout his writings he used a number of key images. Some of them appear in the poems in this selection.

Countryside, forests, trees

He saw the open fields before the agricultural revolution as a landscape of innocence; people were free to roam where they wished, without barriers. In eighteenth century Britain most forests either belonged to the King, or to wealthy and powerful men, whom Blake saw as oppressors of ordinary people. Forests were enclosed, dark and hidden places. To William Blake they represented the opposite of the open landscape of freedom and innocence.

As you will see in 'A Poison Tree' and 'The Human Abstract', he uses the image of the single tree to communicate powerful feelings about human behaviour. The tree – like the tree of knowledge in the Garden of Eden in the Bible – stood for mystery and secret knowledge.

Gardens, enclosed places

The open countryside meant freedom and innocence; the world of nature was readily available to everybody. People who fenced it off made secret places in which dark and evil actions could take place away from public view. We usually think of gardens as attractive, friendly places, but Blake saw them as threatening and secret. It was in the Garden of Eden that Adam and Eve were tempted by the fruit of the Tree of Knowledge, lost their innocence and were rejected by God.

Stars

In Blake's time people believed that the stars could 'damage your health' by their influence. For this and other reasons Blake saw them as a symbol of everything that oppressed human beings and took away their freedom; especially as an image of war and human aggression.

Reading with imagination

Although these images are described as symbols, you should not think that reading Blake's poems is a matter of cracking a code. You need to read the poems with imagination and allow the images to work in your mind. Although the tree had a symbolic importance for William Blake, in 'A Poison Tree' and 'The Human Abstract', he used it in different ways, as you will see when you read them.

A Poison Tree

I was angry with my friend:
I told my wrath, my wrath did end.
I was angry with my foe:
I told it not, my wrath did grow.

5   And I watered it in fears,
Night and morning with my tears;
And I sunned it with smiles,
And with soft deceitful wiles.

And it grew both day and night,
10   Till it bore an apple bright;
And my foe beheld it shine,
And he knew that it was mine,

And into my garden stole
When the night had veiled the pole:
15   In the morning glad I see
My foe outstretched beneath the tree.

Explanations

wrath: anger
veiled the pole: hidden the Pole
   (north) Star

Exploring the poem

One way of starting to think about a poem is to write notes on it – marking words and sections and jotting down the ideas that come into your head as you think about them.

title helps us know what he's talking about early on in the poem

A Poison Tree

I was angry with my friend:
I told my wrath, my wrath did end.
I was angry with my foe:
I told it not, my wrath did grow.

5 And I watered it in fears,
Night and morning with my tears;
And I sunned it with smiles,
And with soft deceitful wiles.

And it grew both day and night,
10 Till it bore an apple bright;
And my foe beheld it shine,
And he knew that it was mine,

And into my garden stole
When the night had veiled the pole:
15 In the morning glad I see
My foe outstretched beneath the tree.

is he talking about just ordinary friends – everyday situations? – or something more?

tears and smiles because of wrath? – happy and sad because he's making his anger grow?

it's like the tree of knowledge in the Garden of Eden . . . but that tree belonged to God – so is he saying he is like God was when Adam and Eve were tempted?

so the enemy knows he's 'growing' his anger – and wants one of his own?

so the enemy goes to steal it?

does it really mean Pole Star? Night doesn't hide stars – it makes it possible to see them.

Thinking about the poem

1 Do you think it is true that if you are angry with a friend and talk about it, the anger ends?
2 Do people deliberately feed their anger with enemies?
3 Which of these statements is the best description of the poem, and why?
   - It is an account of how someone killed an enemy.
   - It shows how the power of evil is part of human nature.
   - It describes how we can choose to do good or evil.
   - It describes the end of a friendship.

Writing about the poem

You have spent some time reading and thinking about this poem. Now write down your thoughts and feelings about it. Don't worry about making it a very organised piece of writing – just write down your ideas as they come to you.

Keep this piece of writing for later reference.

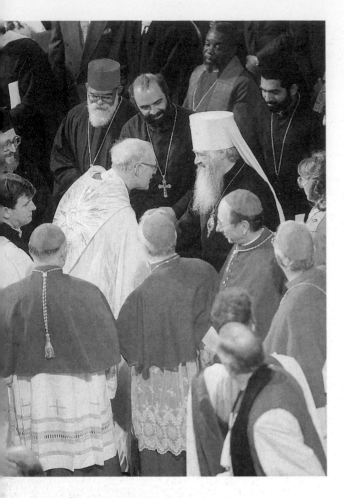

The Human Abstract

Pity would be no more
If we did not make somebody Poor;
And Mercy no more could be
If all were as happy as we.

5   And mutual fear brings peace,
Till the selfish loves increase:
Then Cruelty knits a snare
And spreads his baits with care.

He sits down with holy fears
10   And waters the ground with tears:
Then Humility takes its root
Underneath his foot.

Commentary

In *Songs of Innocence*, William Blake wrote a poem called 'The Divine Image'. This is a positive statement of the way in which human goodness is the image of the goodness of God:

> *For Mercy, Pity, Peace, and Love*
> *Is God, our father dear,*
> *And Mercy, Pity, Peace, and Love*
> *Is Man, his child and care.*

The poem shows us the other side of human nature. Blake tells us that Pity and Mercy only need to exist because of the ways in which human beings treat each other.

Key images

Tree, Mystery: for an explanation of these images, see the notes on page 7
Catterpiller: an image that Blake uses more than once – the worm or grub that burrows into the heart of something beautiful and destroys it from inside
Raven: image of death

*E*xplanations

Human Abstract: summary of what a human being is
mutual fear: fear of each other
knits a snare: makes a trap
Deceit: misleading someone by concealing the truth
Ruddy: red

Soon spreads the dismal shade
Of Mystery over his head;
15 And the Catterpiller and Fly
Feed on the Mystery.

And it bears the fruit of Deceit,
Ruddy and sweet to eat;
And the Raven his nest has made
20 In its thickest shade.

The Gods of the earth and sea,
Sought thro' Nature to find this Tree;
But their search was all in vain:
There grows one in the Human Brain.

Exploring the poem

Write a set of notes on the poem, following
the pattern on page 9.

Thinking about the poem

1   Can you think of examples of what
    Blake is saying in lines 1–2 and 3–4?
2   What does he mean by line 5? Is he
    right?
3   What is Cruelty trying to trap with his
    'snare' and 'baits'?
4   If Cruelty is trying to trap something or
    someone, what should we think of his
    'holy fears' and 'tears'? Are they real?
    Or pretend?
5   What picture do you see from lines
    13–16? What feelings does it give you?

6   Do lines 17–18 remind you of anything?
    What does this verse add to the poem as
    a whole?
7   What do you think Blake is saying about
    human nature in this poem? Would it be
    true to say that he is very pessimistic?

Writing about the poem

Write two or three paragraphs expressing
your thoughts and feelings about the poem.

London

I wander thro' each chartered street,
Near where the chartered Thames does flow,
And mark in every face I meet
Marks of weakness, marks of woe.

5   In every cry of every man,
In every infant's cry of fear,
In every voice, in every ban
The mind-forged manacles I hear.

How the chimney-sweeper's cry
10 Every blackening church appalls;
And the hapless soldier's sigh
Runs in blood down palace walls.

But most thro' midnight streets I hear
How the youthful harlot's curse
15 Blasts the new born infant's tear,
And blights with plagues the marriage hearse.

*E*xplanations

chartered: a charter is a document giving rights and privileges to a person or organisation. In the past they were usually awarded by the King and were often granted to wealthy or powerful people in return for money or support. Here Blake means 'full of privilege' (but only for the rich, of course)

mark: notice

mind-forged manacles: chains that are made ('forged') in people's minds

chimney-sweeper: a young boy who had to climb up inside chimneys in order to clean them

hapless: unlucky

soldier: at the time Blake was writing, the government had brought soldiers into London to prevent a revolution

youthful harlot: young prostitute

blights: withers, spoils

plagues: diseases

hearse: vehicle that carries a coffin to a funeral

Looking at the whole poem

1 How does Blake picture himself at the start of the poem?
2 What details of the city does he focus on?
3 Which words or phrases struck you most vividly as you read the poem?
4 How would you describe the feelings Blake expresses in the poem?

Looking at the detail

5 Why do you think William Blake describes the streets and even the River Thames as 'chartered'?
6 What does he see and hear as he walks (lines 3–7)?
7 The first two verses build up to line 8: 'The mind-forged manacles I hear.' What is Blake saying about the society he is observing?
8 Lines 9–12 add details of what he sees. Explain:
   a) the details Blake observes
   b) his comments on them.
9 What does Blake hear in the 'midnight streets'? What is his comment on this?
10 Look back at your answer to question 7. How do the third and fourth verses change or develop Blake's picture of society?

Looking at the images

Each of the following images is in the poem. As you look at each one make a picture in your mind of what it describes. Then write down a description of what you see or hear.

- 'in every face . . . marks of woe'
- 'the infant's cry of fear'
- 'the hapless soldier's sigh'
- 'blood down palace walls'
- 'the marriage hearse'.

Writing

Imaginative

1 Write a poem, description or short story using one of these titles:
   - Through midnight streets
   - Blood on the palace walls.
2 Suppose Blake were alive now. Think about what he might observe in a modern city and how he might react. Write his description of a journey through the streets of London or another large city and his feelings about it.

About the poem

Look back over your responses to the ten questions about the poem. Write three or four paragraphs about what it says and your reactions to it. You might follow this plan:
a) an explanation of what the writer has observed
b) the feelings he expresses about what he has seen and heard
c) examples of how he uses language to create vivid pictures in our minds
d) a statement of your reactions to the poem.

The Lamb

Little Lamb, who made thee?
Dost thou know who made thee?
Gave thee life, and bid thee feed,
By the stream and o'er the mead?
5   Gave thee clothing of delight,
Softest clothing, woolly, bright?
Gave thee such a tender voice,
Making all the vales rejoice?
Little Lamb, who made thee?
10   Dost thou know who made thee?

Little Lamb, I'll tell thee,
Little Lamb, I'll tell thee:
He is called by thy name,
For he calls himself a Lamb.
15   He is meek, and he is mild;
He became a little child.
I a child, and thou a lamb,
We are called by his name.
Little Lamb, God bless thee!
20   Little Lamb, God bless thee!

Explanations

mead: meadow, field
vales: valleys
called: pronounced with two
  syllables: 'call - edd'

The Tiger

Tiger! Tiger! burning bright
In the forests of the night,
What immortal hand or eye
Could frame thy fearful symmetry?

5   In what distant deeps or skies
Burnt the fire of thine eyes?
On what wings dare he aspire?
What the hand dare seize the fire?

And what shoulder, and what art,
10   Could twist the sinews of thy heart ?
And when thy heart began to beat,
What dread hand, and what dread feet ?

What the hammer? what the chain?
In what furnace was thy brain?
15   What the anvil? what dread grasp
Dare its deadly terrors clasp?

When the stars threw down their spears,
And water'd heaven with their tears,
Did he smile his work to see?
20   Did he who made the Lamb make thee ?

Tiger! Tiger! burning bright
In the forests of the night,
What immortal hand or eye
Dare frame thy fearful symmetry?

Explanations

frame: shape, make
fearful: terrifying

Thinking about animals

Like many of us, Blake looked at animals and then thought about people. Try it.

1   What human qualities does each of these creatures suggest to you?
    ● a snake
    ● a koala bear
    ● a porpoise
    ● a wasp.
2   Which animal would you choose to represent these human qualities?
    ● anger
    ● innocence
    ● power
    ● weakness.

'The Tiger': a group reading

One of the first things that you notice when you read this poem is its powerful rhythm. The pattern of sounds made by the poem is an important part of its impact.

Work out an effective reading of the poem for 3, 4, or 5 voices. Try reading it in different ways to see how to get the best effect. Remember:
● you need to do justice to the sounds and rhythms of the poem
● however you read the poem, it must still make sense
● it is made up of questions
● it moves from the question in lines 3 and 4 to the question in lines 23 and 24. Find ways of showing this in your reading.

The poems as a whole

The lamb

What has struck Blake about the lamb? Look at the poem again and make a list of the qualities he describes. Some of the words you need are in the poem itself; others are suggested by them.

The tiger

Now do the same for the tiger.

Contrasts

What contrasts do the two poems bring out:
● between the two animals?
● between the different ways in which Blake believes human beings can behave?

Who is 'he'?

Both the poems refer to 'he'. Find the references in each one. William Blake's picture of God and the creation of the world was taken from Christianity, but it differed from the teachings of the churches. These are some possible explanations of who 'he' may be in the poems:
● Jesus Christ
● the forgiving God of the New Testament
● the vengeful God of the Old Testament
● some other god who created the world and who is behind all the religions.

What impression do you have from these two poems of what Blake means by 'he'?

Writing about both poems

1   Explain what Blake finds strange about:
    ● the tiger
    ● the lamb.
    What are the most important differences between the tiger and the lamb as they are shown in Blake's poems?
2   What contrasting ideas can you find in 'The Lamb' and 'The Tiger'? In your answer you should consider:
    ● what the ideas are
    ● how he presents them.

Thinking about the exam

The examiner will either:
- ask you to write about particular poems, or
- ask you to write about a topic or theme and choose the poems to refer to.

In either case, you will have to write about two or more poems that are grouped in some way.

Linking the poems

There is only a limited number of ways in which you can link the poems. The most likely are:
- subject matter
- how the poems are written
- personal choice.

Subject

Each of the poems tackles one or more themes that were of particular importance to Blake. Complete this chart by putting a tick against each poem which deals with each subject.

	The Tiger	The Lamb	Poison Tree	Human Abstract	London
power	✔				✔
love		✔			
beauty					
hatred			✔		
friendship					
pity					
oppression					
innocence					
experience					
sin					

Add any more subjects which you can think of and tick them too.

Now sort out what you could say about each subject using the work you have done on the poems already. Look for similarities and differences in the way subjects are treated in the poems.

Working with this chart should help you sort out which poems you could use to discuss any subject in an exam question.

How the poems are written

We can also talk and write about how the poems are written. You will have done this as you read and discussed the poems. For example you will have thought about:
- **imagery and symbolism** – these are both explained in the *Glossary* at the end of the book. There is also more information about Blake's use of images and symbols on page 7.

- **language** – Blake's writing often seems very simple; he doesn't use a lot of long or complicated words. But his choice of words allows him to create a powerful impact. Look carefully at how he does this.
- **the pattern of the poems –** these poems use regular rhythm and rhyme (see the *Glossary* for more about this). This makes them different from most of the other poems in this book. Although it was traditional to write in this way in Blake's time, he makes these *forms* work for him. Look, for example at the way he creates a powerful rhythmic drive in 'The Tiger'.

Make sure that:
- you understand clearly what each of these means (see *Glossary* page 95)
- you can think of good examples of each.

You can mark these in your copy of the *Anthology* in preparation for the examination.

Personal choice

The examiner may ask you to write about two or three poems that you have chosen yourself and may ask you why you have chosen them (like question 2 below). Or you may be asked to think of poems that have a common theme and write about them (like questions 3, 5, and 6 below).

Sample questions

Foundation Tier

1   Write about two of Blake's poems that have interested you. Think about:
- his ideas and attitudes
- his choice of words
- the sound of his poems
- how the poems are set out.

2   In some of his poems, Blake expresses strong feelings about the society he lives in. Write about two poems that do this. You could comment on:
- the subject he writes about
- the feelings he expresses about it
- the pictures he makes to get across his feelings
- the language he uses.

3   Blake was an artist as well as a poet. Choose two poems which show how he created vivid pictures in his writing. Select images from the poems and explain what they depict and how they contribute to the impact of the poem.

Higher Tier

1   Choose two poems in which Blake conveys strong feelings. Write about the way he conveys these feelings through the poems. You should comment on:
- the language he uses
- imagery and symbolism
- rhythm
- form.

2   In what ways do you think Blake was a critic of his society? Choose two poems in which he attacks contemporary society and comment on:
- the aspects of society he attacks
- the imagery and language he uses
- the impact the poems have.

3   Blake's poems often seem very simple on the surface, but underneath they are far from simple. Choose two poems that you discovered more about as you read them. Describe what you see 'beneath the surface' of these poems.

2 Gillian Clarke

—— Her life ——

Gillian Clarke is one of the most popular Welsh poets of today. Yet no one might ever have read any of her poems. All her early poems, written after she left college, she threw in the waste paper bin – she did not feel they were worth keeping. But one of them was picked out of the bin without her knowledge, sent to a poetry magazine and published. That was the start. Even today, there are perhaps nine poems hidden in her notebooks for every poem that she agrees to publish.

Gillian was born in Cardiff in 1937 and brought up there. She was a talented student and went to University College, Cardiff, to take an English degree. Apart from two years working for the BBC in London, she has lived in Wales all her life, earning her living as a writer.

She writes essentially about Wales, especially its landscapes and its rural life. More generally, her poems consider the rhythm of the seasons. Earlier poems also reflect her life in a city and as a mother bringing up three children in the suburbs of Cardiff.

These days she lives where the views are probably as breathtaking as anywhere in the world: a remote hillside cottage in west Wales. Take a short walk from her cottage and you can see the peaks of three great mountains. It is a remote and peaceful place with water coming from the cottage's own well and electricity from its own windmill. In the fields around her home are her sheep. This is the land her father came from, although Gillian was brought up in the city. It is not all beauty and peace: the weather can be harsh and wild and the Air Force pilots practising flying low over the hills often shatter the peace of a quiet afternoon.

Inspirations

The way Gillian Clarke writes has remained similar since the beginning. She claims that she can start writing 'anywhere' and always carries a black felt pen and a pad of paper. Once she has started, she looks for somewhere with complete silence. Noises that can get in the way include 'a radio playing in the next room' or 'the background hum of machinery'. It is not surprising to discover that she does not write poems using a computer – although it is used later to produce a typed copy.

For her, a poem begins with 'two ideas coming together'. The flash of inspiration is the connection between one thing and another. When it happens, it feels like a 'brilliant idea': the hard work is in turning it into a good poem. These days she works in primary schools and writes for children for the BBC. She says that, 'it helps that I work for young children because it forces me to keep my writing simple.' Every time she re-drafts her work, she is trying to make it clearer, more open to the reader, less elaborate. That remains true whether it is a story for five year olds or a poem for an adult audience. In school, Gillian Clarke was good at art as well as English. Although she never developed that skill, she feels that 'my writing is my drawing.'

Her poetry is a part of her culture and her country but it also reflects the tensions of life in Wales. Gillian is Welsh but differs from her father because her first language is English. She chooses to write in the language she grew up with but, as an adult, she has become bi-lingual. In Cardiff, English was the language that was usually spoken. In the hill country where she now lives, it is Welsh. She also reflects the contrast in Wales between the countryside and town. Most Welsh people live in its towns and cities, a large percentage of them in the south. However, the greatest part of the land and the beauty of Wales is in remote rural places, where jobs are scarce and young people frequently have to leave in order to gain work.

Gillian Clarke is distinctly a Welsh poet. England is another country and her sense of national identity is as strong as any writer who helps to make up the multi-cultural tradition of writing in English.

Her work

To get a fuller sense of her work, you could read these poems:
- 'Blaen Cwrt' (written about the cottage she bought as a derelict shell and where she now lives)
- 'At One Thousand Feet' (about living at the cottage now)
- 'Swinging'

- 'Catrin' (about her daughter)
- 'Lament' (written at the time of the Gulf War and the poem she would recommend to be read alongside 'The Field-Mouse')
- 'Miracle on St David's Day'
- 'Suicide on Pentwyn Bridge'
- 'Cofiant' (the long poem of which 'Wil Williams' is part)
- 'Babysitting'
- 'Letter from a Far Country' (a difficult poem but it gives a sense of her life and the world as seen through her eyes).

Poetry books by Gillian Clarke

The Sundial, Carcanet Press, 1985
Letter from a Far Country, Carcanet Press, 1982
Selected Poems, Carcanet Press, 1985
Letting in the Rumour, Carcanet Press, 1989
The King of Britain's Daughter, Carcanet Press, 1993
Collected Poems, Carcanet Press

Wil Williams

'Wil Williams' is part of a long poem called 'Cofiant' which is Welsh for biography or life story. It is part of Gillian Clarke's exploration of her family and her roots. Wil was her grandfather, although she did not know him personally because he died before she was born.

Wil Williams
(1861–1910)

He kept a garden
like other railwaymen
in that old world of the Great Western.
When his daughter went back
5   It disappointed her.
How sad, she said,
to see my mother's house so shabby,
the yard-hens scraggy,
the stackyard sour with old hay,
10   the house dirty.
I can't see the house in her mind,
only the white farm on the hill
that is still there.
Down through the tunnels along the line
15   they run away from us,
the rooms, the women who tended them,
the dressers of glinting jugs,
the lines of sweet washing between trees.
The stations with their cabbage-patches
20   and tubbed geraniums are closed
and the trains' long cries are swallowed
in the throats of tunnels.

Explanations

Great Western: the railway company that served Wales and the West of England

scraggy: thin (so not of the best quality)

stackyard: a yard where hay or corn is piled up and kept

dressers: big kitchen cupboards (the bottom part like a sideboard and the top part for displaying plates and other items)

sweet: sweet smelling

tubbed geraniums: flowers in large outdoor pots

What sort of poem?

Which of these is the best description of the poem? Why?

a) A poem about someone who worked on the railway.

b) A poem about going back to a place and being disappointed.

c) A poem about memories.

Looking at the detail

1 What did the daughter (Gillian Clarke's aunt) find when she returned to her father's house?

2 What does Gillian Clarke herself see of the scene from the past?

3 What does she imagine about the women who once lived there?

4 What has happened to the railway?

The pictures in the poem

You have been asked to describe to an illustrator how to illustrate this poem using just three pictures. Describe what you would want to be drawn or painted.

Explain it as carefully as you can so the illustrator can understand from your words what you see in the poem.

Writing

Imaginative

1 Write your own poem about one or more of your relatives. Include:
- where they live (or lived)
- what they do (or did)
- what people think of them
- what changes have happened since they were young.

Try to include your family's views or memories about them as well as your own. If there is no one in the family who you want to write about, choose another person you know well.

About the poem

2 Look back at your answers to the four questions about the poem. Write three or four paragraphs about your responses. These should include:
- what the poem suggests to you as a whole
- a closer look at each verse
- comments on words and phrases that you think are particularly effective
- your own reactions to the poem.

Jac Codi Baw

They have torn down in the space of time
it takes to fill a shopping bag,
the building that stood beside my car.
It was grown over with ragwort,
5   toadflax and buddleia, windows
blind with boarding. Other cars
had time to drive away. Mine
is splattered with the stones' blood, smoky
with ghosts. We are used to the slow
10   change that weather brings, the gradual
death of a generation, old bricks
crumbling. Inside the car dust lies,
grit in my eyes, in my hair.

He doesn't care. It's a joke to him
15   clearing space for the pile-drivers,
cheerful in his yellow machine,
cat-calling, laughing at my grief.
But for him too the hand-writing
of a city will be erased.
20   I can't laugh. Too much comes down
in the deaths of warehouses. Brickdust,
shards of Caernarfon slate. Blood on our hands.

Explanations

Jac Codi Baw: The words are Welsh and literally mean 'Jack raises the dirt'. People started using them as a nickname for the massive yellow earth moving machines which had the letters J.C.B. on them. From there it has passed into more general use in the language – it is now used to describe any large earth mover.

ragwort, toadflax and buddleia: flowers

erased: rubbed out, removed

shards: small, sharp, brittle pieces

What has happened?

'Jac Codi Baw' describes an incident in the poet's life.
Explain what has happened in as much detail as the poem allows.

Looking at the images

Look at these images from the poem.
As you look at each one, think about the pictures it creates in your mind and what it suggests to you. Write down what you think and see.

- 'splattered with the stones' blood'
- 'smoky with ghosts'
- 'for him too the hand-writing of a city will be erased'
- 'Too much comes down in the deaths of warehouses'
- 'Blood on our hands'.

How she feels

The poet obviously feels differently about the demolition of buildings from the person operating the JCB. However, it is not simply of matter of one person being for it and one against it. Look at these statements about the poet's views.

- a) Clarke finds it hard to come to terms with change.
- b) Clarke feels guilty about the destruction of old buildings.
- c) Clarke is concerned about the speed of change.
- d) Clarke is obsessed about keeping old buildings.
- e) Clarke is concerned that demolition destroys the character of a place.
- f) Clarke is concerned about what the ghosts that are released will do.

- Which statements do you think are accurate and why?
- Which ones are misleading and why?
- Choose the one that you think best describes her response to the situation and explain your choice.

Writing

Imaginative

1 Imagine you are the JCB operator and you have watched the scene described in the poem. Describe the incident from your point of view.
2 Imagine you are the poet and decide to write to the local newspaper about the redevelopment taking place in Carnarfon. What do you write?

About the poem

3 Write about the way Clarke creates a sense of the damage caused by the demolition. Think about:
- the speed of the demolition
- the attitude of the demolition worker
- vivid words and phrases
- the contrast between natural decay and man-made demolition.

No Hands

War-planes have been at it all day long
shaking the world, strung air
humming like pianos when children bang the keys

over and over; willow warbler song
5   and jet planes; lads high on speed up there
in a mindless thrum; down here a brake of trees

churns to a rolling wave and there's no let
in the after-quiver along air-waves struck
by silly boys who think they strum guitars,

10   who skim the fields like surfboards over crests
of hedges, where a tractor swims in a green wake
of grass dust tossed to dry under sun and stars:

boy scaring boy off the face of his own land,
all do and dare, and look at me, no hands.

Explanations

willow warbler: small bird that arrives
from Africa in the spring; known for
its beautiful singing voice; unusual
because it often sings as it flies

thrum: humming

brake of trees: a small group of trees
planted as protection against the
wind

churns: moves violently this way and
that

let: let up

after-quiver: shaking that goes on after
the event

crests: tops (the word is used because the
hedges seem to be used like waves
are for surfboards)

Looking at the whole poem

1 What has been happening during the day described in this poem?
2 What effects do the planes have?

Looking at each verse

3 What is the most important feeling that Clarke gets across in the first verse?
4 What contrasts with the noise of the plane in the second verse?
5 With what are the Air Force pilots compared in the third verse?
6 What picture of the pilots is offered in the fourth verse?
7 What is being emphasised in the final couplet?

Looking at the words

8 Here are three of the ways that Clarke describes the pilots:
   ● 'lads high on speed up there'
   ● 'silly boys'
   ● 'all do and dare, and look at me, no hands'.
   a) What pictures and connections are created in your mind by these phrases and what is the overall effect?
   b) What other phrases would you pick out to help complete the picture of the pilots? Explain why you have chosen them.
9 Look back at the first two verses and pick out all the ways in which the noise made by the planes is emphasised. Write about the effect created by the words and phrases you have chosen.

Looking at the form

The poem is a sonnet (see *Glossary* page 96), the traditional form used for love poetry. The poem does not follow a strict rhyme scheme or follow a strictly regular rhythmic pattern. Why do you think the poet might have chosen this form and used it in this way?

Writing

Imaginative

1 Write your own poem in which something intrudes into your normal day. It could be:
   ● repair work in school
   ● road works
   ● decorating at home
   ● someone with a noisy stereo
   ● electric lawnmowers.
   You could try to use the sonnet form in the way that Gillian Clarke has done.

About the poem

2 A couple of friends have asked you what you think Clarke feels about low flying planes and their pilots. How would you answer them? Think especially about:
   ● the noise
   ● the effects of the flying
   ● the descriptions of the pilots.
3 Look back over the responses to the poem which you gave to the nine questions opposite. Write three or four paragraphs about the poem. These should include:
   a) what the planes do
   b) how the pilots and their flying are described
   c) how the poet expresses her view of the low flying planes
   d) your reactions to the poem.

Sunday

Getting up early on a Sunday morning
leaving them sleep for the sake of peace,
the lunch pungent, windows open
for a blackbird singing in Cyncoed.
5   Starlings glistening in the gutter come
for seed. I let the cats in from the night,
their fur already glossed and warm with March.
I bring the milk, newspaper, settle here
in the bay of the window to watch people
10   walking to church for Mothering Sunday.
A choirboy holds his robes over his shoulder.
The cats jump up on windowsills to wash
and tremble at the starlings. Like peaty water
sun slowly fills the long brown room.
15   Opening the paper I admit to this
the war-shriek and starved stare
of a warning I can't name.

Explanations

pungent: filling the air with its smell
Cyncoed: a suburb of Cardiff, the capital
    city of Wales
glistening: shining, gleaming
glossed: shiny
tremble: to shake, not with fear in this
    case but with the excitement of the
    possible chase
peaty: stained dark brown

Looking at the whole poem

1 What family situation is described at the start of this poem?
2 What does Clarke do in the poem?
3 What time of year is described?
4 What do we learn about the weather?
5 What does Clarke watch from the window?
6 What sort of stories does she find in the newspaper?

Looking further

7 This is one of Clarke's earlier poems written when she lived in a city. In what ways does the poem reflect a sensitivity to things more likely to be associated with rural life?
8 Write about the way the last two lines of the poem link up with the first two lines.
9 What, in your view, is the effect of the way the poem finishes?

Writing

Descriptive

1 Write your own description of a morning where you live. Try to include a range of sights and sounds as Gillian Clarke does.

Imaginative

2 Write a short story called 'Sunday'. For example, your story could start peacefully and then the quiet is shattered by something that happens.

About the poem

3 What impression do you have of Clarke's Sunday morning from reading her poem? Consider:
  ● what she does
  ● what she sees
  ● the effect of opening the newspaper.

4 Look back over your responses to the poem from the earlier questions. Write three or four paragraphs about the poem. These should include:
  ● a description of the situation
  ● words and phrases that help to make the scene come alive
  ● a comment about the contrast between what the poet sees around her and what she sees in the newspaper
  ● your reaction to the poem.

The Field-Mouse

Summer, and the long grass is a snare drum.
The air hums with jets.
Down at the end of the meadow,
far from the radio's terrible news,
5 we cut the hay. All afternoon
its wave breaks before the tractor blade.
Over the hedge our neighbour travels his field
in a cloud of lime, drifting our land
with a chance gift of sweetness.

10 The child comes running through the killed flowers,
his hands a nest of quivering mouse,
its black eyes two sparks burning.
We know it will die and ought to finish it off.
It curls in agony big as itself
15 and the star goes out in its eye.
Summer in Europe, the field's hurt,
and the children kneel in long grass,
staring at what we have crushed.

Before day's done the field lies bleeding,
20 the dusk garden inhabited by the saved, voles,
frogs, a nest of mice. The wrong that woke
from a rumour of pain won't heal,
and we can't face the newspapers.
All night I dream the children dance in grass
25 their bones brittle as mouse-ribs, the air
stammering with gunfire, my neighbour turned
stranger, wounding my land with stones.

Explanations

jets: planes

radio's terrible news: the poem was written during the war in Bosnia in which ordinary people were shot and bombed day after day

wave: the movement of the hay

lime: an alkaline substance that farmers sometimes use to improve their soil

quivering: shaking with fear

dusk: after sunset when darkness is falling

inhabited: lived in

brittle: hard but easily broken

stammering: literally it means stuttering – failing to get the words out clearly. Here it suggests the repetitive sound of gunfire

my neighbour turned stranger: in the dream the neighbour has become part of the Bosnian war situation

Looking at the verses

1 Look at the first verse. What work is the poet involved in?

2 What does one of the children do in the second verse?

3 Look at the third verse. What is gathered in the garden at the end of the day?

4 Look at the dream in the third verse. What sort of dream is it and what does it add to the poem?

Looking at the images

5 Look at these phrases from the poem. As you look at each one, think about the pictures it creates in your mind and what it suggests to you. Write down what you think and see.
- 'the long grass is a snare drum'
- 'The air hums with jets'
- 'through the killed flowers'
- 'It curls in agony big as itself'
- 'the field lies bleeding'
- 'their bones brittle as mouse-ribs'.

Looking at the whole poem

The poem brings together two things: harvest in Wales and war in Bosnia.

6 Make a note of all the references to the Bosnian situation.

7 Make a note of all the words and phrases that connect the harvest with the war.

8 Read the poem again and decide what is the overall effect of these two aspects of the poem. To help you, here are three reactions to the poem:
- Gillian Clarke is haunted by the news of war and it keeps showing through.
- The poem is unusual because harvest and war are normally seen as being very different.
- The poem shows how close death is even in the most peaceful of scenes.

Writing

Imaginative

1 Write about a situation where you try to save something or someone. What happens? Think up your own story or develop one of these situations:
- trying to get your parents to give a home to an unwanted kitten or puppy
- trying to save a friend from being punished
- trying to save an open space or park near your home.

2 Write a dream sequence in which things that are a regular part of your life become strange and horrible. The dream might include home, school, friends and family: in your dream nothing happens normally and you have no control over the situation.

About the poem

3 Look back over your responses to the poem in the earlier questions. Write three or four paragraphs about the poem. You should include:
- comments about each verse
- comments about the way language is used
- a response to the poem as a whole.

4 Write about how Clarke communicates a sense of guilt for the damage that the harvesting does to the wildlife. Think about:
- the effect of individual phrases and images
- the role of the children in the poem
- the role of the news about war
- the way the poem ends
- your reactions to the poem.

Thinking about the exam

The examiner will not tell you the questions in advance but there need not be any big surprises. The examiner might ask you to write about:

- an individual poem
- two poems and compare them (it could be three poems, but that is less likely)
- all of Gillian Clarke's poems in the *Anthology*
- a subject that links some of the poems (in which case you may be asked to choose the poems you write about)
- your choice from the five poems in the *Anthology*.

Linking the poems

1   The links between the poems are many. Here are some suggestions. Complete them by adding the linked poem(s).
(Poems can be referred to more than once.)

- Views of the city: 'Jac Codi Baw' and ...
- Views of country life: 'No Hands' and ...
- Family life: 'Sunday' and ...
- Change: 'Jac Codi Baw' and ...
- War and violence intruding on peace: 'No Hands', 'Sunday' and ...
- Over-confident young men: 'No Hands' and ...
- A sense of threat: 'The Field-Mouse' and ....

2   Can you see any other links? What are they?

3   Which of all these links do you think are the strongest?
Clearly, the stronger the link, the more likely that it will appear in the examination. At the same time, remember that any link could form the basis of a question.

How the poems are written

It is important to write about how the poems are written and not just what happens in them. You will have done this as you discussed the poems, worked on them and answered questions about them. For example, you will have thought about:

- **imagery** – this includes metaphor and simile. You need to say what the language does. For example, it is not helpful to say that in 'Jac Codi Baw' 'stones' blood' is a metaphor. It is helpful to say that 'stones' blood' gives the sense that there is more than bricks and dust being demolished, that the building has had a life which is now being destroyed.
- **use of language** – this covers imagery, but includes all the ways in which language carries meaning. For example, calling the Air Force pilots 'silly boys' in 'No Hands' makes them sound like primary school children.

- **form** – the most obvious aspect of form is the way the poem is divided into lines and verses. It gives you a natural (and easy!) way to start considering a poem. Remember that 'No Hands' is written in sonnet form.
- **verse or stanza** – sometimes it helps to give each stanza a name or heading as you prepare so you are reminded of what occurs in each part of the poem.

Make sure that:
- you understand clearly what each of these means (see *Glossary* page 95)
- you can think of good examples of each.

You can mark these in your copy of the *Anthology* in preparation for the examination.

Even more important than knowing technical words is understanding what effect the choice of language has.

Sample questions

Foundation Tier

1 Write about two of Gillian Clarke's poems that create a particularly strong picture in your mind. You might want to write about:
- her choice of words
- how the poems are set out
- differences between the two poems
- the overall effect of the poems.

2 Write about the people and situations described in:
a) 'Jac Codi Baw'
and
b) 'No Hands'.
Think especially about:
- what the demolition worker and the pilots are doing
- how the poet feels about their work.

3 Which poems by Gillian Clarke give you the strongest sense of what she is describing? You should think about:
- what she is describing
- how she feels about what she describes
- the way she uses particular words and phrases
- your feelings about what she describes.

Higher Tier

1 Write about two poems by Gillian Clarke which strongly create a sense of place for you. In your answer you should reflect upon:
- her use of imagery
- her feelings about the places
- how the form of the poem affects your response
- similarities and differences between the poems.

2 'Gillian Clarke's poetry gives the impression of someone who is uncomfortable with change.' Looking at the poems as a whole, do you agree?

3 Write about the sense of violence that is conveyed in:
a) 'Jac Codi Baw'
and
b) 'The Field-Mouse'.
Look particularly at the way contrasts are used in each poem.

4 '"The Field-Mouse" is a fuller and more successful working out of the theme addressed in Gillian Clarke's earlier poem "Sunday".' What is your response to this view?

3 Seamus Heaney

—— His life ——

Seamus Heaney was born in 1939 in County Derry, in Ireland, at the beginning of the Second World War. He was the eldest of nine children and spent his childhood growing up in the countryside of Mossbawn, on his father's fifty acre farm. Although technology had advanced greatly in the early twentieth century, traditional farming methods, which had been handed down for generations, were still used on his father's farm. These early memories of farm life gave Heaney much to write about when he was an adult. In the poems which you are studying, he describes, with some admiration, his father's skill in working with the horse-drawn plough in the poem 'Follower'; and he looks at the unsentimental way in which animals were treated on farms in 'The Early Purges'.

Heaney returns to his childhood for many of the memories which form the basis of the poems in this book. In one, he writes very movingly about the experience of being called home from boarding school at the age of 14 to attend a family funeral in 'Mid-Term Break'. The poem records the true story of how Heaney's four year old brother, Christopher, was knocked down in the road and killed, and is written from Heaney's viewpoint, but as if he is the age he was when Christopher died. The young Heaney waits to be collected from school to return home for the funeral. When he arrives back home, he is aware of how the adults around him are trying to cope with the bereavement. The poem ends with a vivid description of how he took part in the custom of going in to see his brother, who was lying in his coffin in a room in the house, before being buried.

—— Growing up ——

Heaney went to the local village school. He passed the eleven-plus examination, so that at twelve he went to boarding school at St. Columb's College, in Derry, which was forty miles away from his home. He did very well at school and went to Queen's University in Belfast to read English where he gained a First Class Honours degree. It was while he was at university that he met his wife, Marie.

When Heaney left university he taught in a secondary school for a year, but he lacked confidence and so did not continue. He became a lecturer at a teacher's training college, and then moved on to became a university lecturer, first at Queen's University where he had studied for his degree. As he has become more successful, he has travelled to lecture in universities in several countries including Harvard in America.

Roots

Heaney's poetry first achieved success in 1966 when *Death of a Naturalist*, the collection from which his poems in this book are taken, was published. Heaney discusses what he felt he was achieving through writing poetry in the poem 'Digging'. He uses the image of digging to explain how, by looking through his past, he can unearth his roots to discover who he is. Describing his father digging flowerbeds leads Heaney to recall childhood scenes when his father dug up new potatoes which had to be collected by the children. It also leads him further back into the past to remember his grandfather digging peat to be burned as fuel on the fire.

Poetic digging allows Heaney to recover things which have been left behind, buried in the 'bog' of his past, which have been preserved by his memory. He is able to re-live what happened, but this time to look at events as an adult who can try to make better sense of what they mean. As a child Heaney was told not to go near the local bog because it was bottomless, but the adult Heaney can dig carefully through and examine the different layers.

Since writing *Death of a Naturalist*, Heaney has produced a number of poetry volumes in which he continues to dig deeper into the bog. While doing so, he gradually moves beyond local and personal reflections to write about wider themes, and to include truths which he feels relate to everyone.

He explores his strong sense of nationality. He does this by looking at the origins of Irish culture: he writes about Irish traditions, legends of Irish saints, and translates Irish epics. He has also written about the modern Irish troubles in Ulster, which is where he continued to live until the beginning of the Seventies. At that time the Irish troubles were particularly turbulent, so Heaney decided to move his family to the Republic of Ireland to live and work in a safer and more peaceful environment.

In 1995 Seamus Heaney's literary achievements were recognised when he won the Nobel Prize for Literature. The award was made 'for works of lyrical beauty and ethical (*moral*) depth which exalt (*show the wonder of*) everyday miracles and the living past'.

He deals with major issues such as life and death; childhood memories; the difference between adults' views and children's; what it is like growing up; rural life; and the past and the present. He uses strong physical images to convey his ideas, and he chooses words which appeal to the senses to make his poems vivid.

Heaney revels in the sounds and rhythms of the words he chooses, as well as in their meanings and associations, so his poems are interesting to hear and to read aloud. He feels that poetry should have energy and passion, and he wants readers to take pleasure from the way language is used even while they are being forced to think.

The Early Purges

I was six when I first saw kittens drown.
Dan Taggart pitched them, 'the scraggy wee shits',
Into a bucket; a frail metal sound,

Soft paws scraping like mad. But their tiny din
5   Was soon soused. They were slung on the snout
Of the pump and the water pumped in.

'Sure isn't it better for them now?' Dan said.
Like wet gloves they bobbed and shone till he sluiced
Them out on the dunghill, glossy and dead.

10   Suddenly frightened, for days I sadly hung
Round the yard, watching the three sogged remains
Turn mealy and crisp as old summer dung

Until I forgot them. But the fear came back
When Dan trapped big rats, snared rabbits, shot crows
15   Or, with a sickening tug, pulled old hens' necks.

Still, living displaces false sentiments
And now, when shrill pups are prodded to drown,
I just shrug, 'Bloody pups'. It makes sense:

'Prevention of cruelty' talk cuts ice in town
20   Where they consider death unnatural,
But on well-run farms pests have to be kept down.

Explanations

Purges: getting rid of things, people or
    animals which are undesirable
scraggy: lean and skinny
soused: drenched in water
snout of the pump: the tube of the water
    pump through which water flows
sluiced: rinsed away
sentiments: feelings

Dramatic reading

When you read the poem aloud, your main aim is to help your listener understand and enjoy the poem. At first you will need to read through the poem carefully several times to make sure that you know what each sentence means.

1   Make notes on where you will need to:
   a) pause for the poem to make sense
   b) use expression in your voice to show what different people in the poem are feeling
   c) bring out the sounds in some words, such as those to do with noises
   d) emphasise rhythms or rhymes to draw attention to words, or create special effects.

2   Practise reading the poem aloud several times before reading it out to your audience.

3   Now listen to the poem being read aloud by someone else.
    Add to your notes any words or phrases which this reader emphasised and you did not.

4   Try to find reasons for each word or phrase chosen for emphasis. You could think about:
   ● the meaning of each word or phrase
   ● what each word sounded like
   ● whether the sounds in that word, or the word itself, were repeated nearby
   ● whether the words were read after a pause (perhaps because of punctuation or a line ending)
   ● any rhythm or sound patterns you heard, and their effect.

The notes you make will help you write about the poem later.

Looking at the whole poem

Immediate reactions

1 Give your views on:
   a) how the animals are treated
   b) how Dan, the farm worker, views the animals
   c) what people from the local town think about what happens to animals on farms.

   Do you think the poet agrees or disagrees with you?

Looking at the people

2 Look closely at the words spoken by people in lines 2, 7, 18 and 19.
   There are two groups of people in the poem: those from the town, and those from the country. Make a chart with two columns, one column for each group of people, and use it to record:
   a) what people from each group say
   b) how people from the two groups speak
   c) what contact people from each group have with the animals
   d) how you think each group believes animals should be treated.

   Can you think of any reasons for the differences you have noted between the two groups?

Changing views

3 Re-read the first five verses which describe Dan Taggart killing the animals. Which words show:
   a) Dan's attitude to what he does?
   b) the young Seamus Heaney's attitude to Dan's actions?

   Whose view do you think you are expected to sympathise with most and why?

4 At the end of the poem Heaney is an adult and his attitude has changed. Why do you think this is? You could think about:
   a) his criticism of town people (line 20)
   b) how Heaney justifies killing the pups
   c) what the 'The Early Purges' are.

5 What does the poem suggest happens when people who live on farms grow up?

6 How does the way the poem is organised bring out the contrast between the six year old and the adult Heaney's reaction to 'pest control'?

The animals

7 The death of the kittens is described using two images:
   'Like wet gloves they bobbed and shone ...'
   '... mealy and crisp as old summer dung'
   Create a picture in your mind of what each describes.
   Explain what each image tells us about the dead kittens. How does it make the reader feel towards them?

8 Heaney describes how all the unwanted animals are killed. Pick out words or phrases which best describe the suffering of each animal. Explain why the words you have chosen are effective.

9 Is the reader encouraged to feel the same about all the animals mentioned in the poem?

Writing

To explain

Imagine that you are an officer for the Royal Society for the Prevention of Cruelty to Animals in the area which includes the farm in the poem. Over the years there have been some complaints about cruelty. You have investigated the farm and looked into:

a) how Dan Taggart gets rid of pests

b) how Seamus Heaney killed the pups.

Other farmers in the area treat animals in a similar way.

Write a letter about 'pest control' explaining to the farmers how you view the way they treat the animals which they call pests and suggesting better ways of dealing with them.

About the poem

1   Write several paragraphs explaining how Heaney describes the people in the poem. You should try to include how he:
    - describes what they do
    - gives them different voices
    - shows their attitudes and feelings towards animals.

2   How does Heaney make us aware that people have different attitudes and feelings about how animals should be treated? You may like to think about:
    - what each group of people in the poem have to say about animals
    - how much experience of animals each group has
    - the way Heaney's attitude towards animals changes in the poem as he grows up.

3   Write three or four paragraphs about the way Heaney makes life on the farm vivid. You could look at:
    - the imagery
    - the language he uses to describe:
        the animals
        their reactions to dying
        their bodies.
    c) how he describes Dan Taggart and himself, and what they do.

Follower

My father worked with a horse-plough,
His shoulders globed like a full sail strung
Between the shafts and the furrow.
The horses strained at his clicking tongue.

5   An expert. He would set the wing
And fit the bright steel-pointed sock.
The sod rolled over without breaking.
At the headrig, with a single pluck

Of reins, the sweating team turned round
10   And back into the land. His eye
Narrowed and angled at the ground,
Mapping the furrow exactly.

I stumbled in his hob-nailed wake,
Fell sometimes on the polished sod;
15   Sometimes he rode me on his back
Dipping and rising to his plod.

I wanted to grow up and plough,
To close one eye, stiffen my arm.
All I ever did was follow
20   In his broad shadow round the farm.

I was a nuisance, tripping, falling,
Yapping always. But today
It is my father who keeps stumbling
Behind me, and will not go away.

Explanations

globed: curved
shafts: the bars between which a horse is harnessed
furrow: the trench made in the ground by a plough
the wing: cuts the bottom of the furrow
the sock: cuts into the soil and turns it
headrig: land at the edge of the field where the
    plough turns round
hob-nailed: with heavy headed nails embedded in
    boot soles to stop them slipping on the mud

Digging

Between my finger and my thumb
The squat pen rests; snug as a gun.

Under my window, a clean rasping sound
When the spade sinks into gravelly ground:
5   My father, digging. I look down

Till his straining rump among the flowerbeds
Bends low, comes up twenty years away
Stooping in rhythm through potato drills
Where he was digging.

10   The coarse boot nestled on the lug, the shaft
Against the inside knee was levered firmly.
He rooted out tall tops, buried the bright edge deep
To scatter new potatoes that we picked
Loving their cool hardness in our hands.

15   By God, the old man could handle a spade.
Just like his old man.

My grandfather cut more turf in a day
Than any other man on Toner's bog.
Once I carried him milk in a bottle
20   Corked sloppily with paper. He straightened up
To drink it, then fell to right away

Nicking and slicing neatly, heaving sods
Over his shoulder, going down and down
For the good turf. Digging.

25   The cold smell of potato mould, the squelch and slap
Of soggy peat, the curt cuts of an edge
Through living roots awaken in my head.
But I've no spade to follow men like them.

Between my finger and my thumb
30   The squat pen rests.
I'll dig with it.

Explanations

digging: as Heaney goes back in time each generation is digging deeper down into the soil. For more explanation of what digging represents look back to page 38

drills: rows of plants

lug: lower part of the spade which is ear shaped and sticks out

shaft: the handle of the spade

tops: the leaves of a plant which is grown for its root

turf: surface soil

Toner's bog: name of a bog (an area of wet spongy ground containing decomposed plant matter, called peat, used for fuel)

curt: short

Dramatic readings

Prepare dramatic readings and make notes on the two poems, ' Follower' and 'Digging', using the method described on page 40 to help you. Try to work out how Seamus Heaney has brought the digging and ploughing to life in the poem.

First impressions

Take each poem in turn and finish these statements:

1 This poem is about …
2 The words or phrases which struck me most were …
3 Heaney is different from his father because …

Changing views

In both poems Heaney is aware of how his views have changed with time.

Decide whether you agree or disagree with the following statements and find proof from the poems to back up your point of view.

The past

- As a child Heaney wanted to be like his father.
- Heaney only admired his father's work on the land.
- The men in Heaney's family have done the same work for generations.

The present

- Heaney's relationship with his father is unchanged at the end of 'Follower'.
- Heaney thinks writing poetry is not as worthwhile as working the land.
- Heaney sees no link between what he does and what his father and grandfather did.

Heaney's father

In the poems 'Follower' and 'Digging' Heaney writes about his father.

1   Look at the image in the first verse of 'Follower':

    His shoulders globed like a full sail strung
    Between the shafts and the furrow

    Make a picture in your mind of what is being described.

    What does the image tell you about the effort involved in ploughing?

2   Which words or phrases in 'Follower' does Heaney use to prove that his father was an 'expert' with the plough?

    You may find it helpful to look at:

    a) technical terms (lines 4–8)
    b) the response of the horses (lines 4 and 8–9)
    c) describing exactly what his father was doing (lines 5–12)

3   What does Heaney say in 'Digging' which reveals his father's skill at digging?

4   Thinking about both poems, how does Heaney make you aware that he admired his father?

Writing

Imaginative

1   Young Heaney's ambition was to grow up to be like his father. Describe someone who, when you were a child, you knew, admired and wanted to be like.

    In your description show why your chosen person was so special.

2   Describe one childhood memory which is particularly important to you and explain how it has led you to become the person you are today.

About the poems

3   Which of the two poems do you find most interesting and why?

    You could think about:

    a) what Heaney is thinking about
    b) his memories and feelings
    c) any words or phrases which appealed to you.

4   Write about the way Heaney presents his relationship with his father in 'Digging' and 'Follower'.

    You may find it helpful to look at:

    a) how he describes his father working on the land
    b) Heaney's changing feelings and attitudes towards him
    c) the way the poems are organised
    d) any images, words or phrases you found effective
    e) how he describes his father at the end of the poem 'Follower'.

5   How effectively does Heaney portray working on the land in these two poems? You could think about:

    a) his choice of images
    b) the technical details he includes
    c) the effects of the sounds and rhythms he uses
    d) any words which appeal to the senses
    e) how he presents the men who worked on the land.

Mid-Term Break

I sat all morning in the college sick bay
Counting bells knelling classes to a close.
At two o'clock our neighbours drove me home.

In the porch I met my father crying –
5 He had always taken funerals in his stride –
And Big Jim Evans saying it was a hard blow.

The baby cooed and laughed and rocked the pram
When I came in, and I was embarrassed
By old men standing up to shake my hand

10 And tell me they were 'sorry for my trouble',
Whispers informed strangers I was the eldest,
Away at school, as my mother held my hand

In hers and coughed out angry tearless sighs.
At ten o'clock the ambulance arrived
15 With the corpse, stanched and bandaged by the nurses.

Next morning I went up into the room. Snowdrops
And candles soothed the bedside; I saw him
For the first time in six weeks. Paler now,

Wearing a poppy bruise on his left temple,
20 He lay in the four foot box as in his cot.
No gaudy scars, the bumper knocked him clear.

A four foot box, a foot for every year.

Explanations

sick bay: the room in the college which you go to when you are ill
knelling: ringing of a funeral bell
stanched: the flow of blood from a wound has been stopped

Dramatic reading

Prepare a dramatic reading of the poem using the method on page 40 to help you.

First impressions

Explain whether these statements are true or false. Use sentences from the poem to prove your answers.

1   The poem is about the death of a younger brother.
2   Both parents are able to comfort Heaney.
3   Heaney is pleased to be recognised as the oldest son by all the neighbours.
4   When Heaney sees his brother's body he is concerned most by the size of the coffin.
5   This poem looks at how people use rituals to help them cope with death.

A closer look

6   Which parts of Heaney's experience strike you most forcibly?
7   Which words or phrases do you think are the most effective?
8   How do the adults in the poem try to make the child's death seem less awful.
9   What does the last line of the poem tell you about death?

Looking at the detail

10   Why is the school bell described as 'knelling'?
11   Three groups of people offer comfort to Heaney in lines 6, 10 and 11.
    a)   How personal are their comments?
    b)   Why do they speak and behave as they do?
    c)   How do their responses compare with Heaney's family's responses ?
12   'the corpse stanched and bandaged by the nurses' (line 15)
    How does this make Heaney's brother seem less familiar?

13   'Wearing a poppy bruise' Make a picture in your mind of what is being described. What does the image tell you about the injury?
14   Look at lines 16–22:
    a)   Which words make us aware of how much Heaney's brother has changed?
    b)   How does the atmosphere Heaney creates at the coffin scene contrast with that of the previous day?

Writing

Imaginative

Should your family, school, and the government treat you as an adult now? Explain how you see teenagers being treated in society and what changes if any you think should be made. You could include:

● legal age limits, for example for driving, drinking and films
● the part adults take in society, for example, voting, in the workforce, involvement in local government
● the rate at which different people mature.

About the poem

1   What effect does the death of Heaney's brother have on him in this poem? You may like to look at how Heaney reacts, what he notices, and how others treat him.
2   In this poem, how does Heaney deal with the experience of a first bereavement? You could think about:
    a)   the boy, Heaney's, experience
    b)   the feelings and behaviour of his family and their friends
    c)   the language used
    d)   what the poem made you think and feel.

Storm on the Island

Before you read the poem, think about what it is about storms which makes them frightening for some people.

We are prepared: we build our houses squat,
Sink walls in rock and roof them with good slate.
The wizened earth has never troubled us
With hay, so, as you can see, there are no stacks
5   Or stooks that can be lost. Nor are there trees
Which might prove company when it blows full
Blast: you know what I mean – leaves and branches
Can raise a tragic chorus in a gale
So that you can listen to the thing you fear
10 Forgetting that it pummels your house too.
But there are no trees, no natural shelter.
You might think that the sea is company,
Exploding comfortably down on the cliffs
But no: when it begins, the flung spray hits
15 The very windows, spits like a tame cat
Turned savage. We just sit tight while wind dives
And strafes invisibly. Space is a salvo,
We are bombarded by the empty air.
Strange, it is a huge nothing that we fear.

The island

Using only the information in the poem to help you:

1 draw and label a diagram of the landscape of the island
2 explain, using details from the poem to help you, whether you would want to live there.

The storm

3 What are the differences between what storms normally do and what happens on this island?
   a) Which experience does the poet show to be worse?
   b) How does he do that?
4 How could trees raise a 'tragic chorus'?
5 How does the poet make you aware that it is unreasonable ever to think of the sea as pleasant? You may like to look at the words 'Exploding comfortably' (line 13) and the image on lines 15 and 16: 'spits like a tame cat turned savage'. Make a picture in your mind of what is being described. What does the image tell you about the sea?
6 What is the effect of using words like 'hits', 'dives', 'strafes', salvo' and 'bombarded' to describe the storm?

Explanations

wizened: dried up
stacks: hay stacks
stooks: a group of twelve corn sheaves stacked up against each other in a field
tragic chorus: a group speaking. Their words either reveal distress, or give a warning about an event they are watching
strafes: a Second World War word describing a gun or bomb attack by a low-flying aircraft
salvo: the firing off of a number of guns or bombs at the same time

More than a storm?

Is the poem just about a storm on an island? Think about:

a) the conflict between the islander and the island with its storms and what it shows about the relationship between human beings and nature
b) the last line of the poem which says 'it is a huge nothing that we fear' (line 19). Write a paragraph exploring what else you think the poem may be about.

Writing

Imaginative

1 Write a story which ends with the words 'it is a huge nothing which we fear'.
2 Describe a place which you know well, and how it alters either during different seasons or because of changing weather.

About the poem

3 What does Heaney tell us which makes life on this island seem particularly difficult?
You could think about:
a) the landscape of the island
b) living conditions on the island
c) what the storms are like.

2 How effectively does Heaney describe the storm on the island?
You could think about:
a) how he describes the islanders being affected by the storm
b) how he describes the storm
c) his use of sounds and imagery
d) your response to the poem.

Thinking about the exam

The examiner will ask you to write in detail about two or more of the poems by:

- naming the poems
- choosing a subject and then asking you to select the best poems to write about
- asking you to choose the poems and to explain your selection.

Linking the poems

The poems can be linked in different ways. The following links are the most likely:

- subject
- how the poems are written.

Subject

Each poem deals with one or more of the topics and themes which matter to Seamus Heaney. Complete this chart by putting a tick against each poem which deals with each subject.

	Follower	Early Purges	Storm	Mid-Term Break	Digging
nature					
country life					
childhood					
adulthood					
growing up					
his family					
his father					
the community					
being a poet					
death					
memories					

Add any more subjects which you can think of and tick them in the same way.

Now sort out what you could say about each subject using the work you have done on the poems already. Look for similarities and differences in the way subjects are treated in the poems.

Working with this chart should help you sort out which poems you could use to discuss any subject in an exam question.

How the poems are written

While reading and discussing the poems, you have already looked at:

- **language** – how some words appeal to the senses, or reveal things about characters
- **imagery** – word pictures such as those describing animals' bodies in 'The Early Purges'
- **sounds** – for example, how these bring to life the wind and the movement of the spade in the soil
- **rhythm** – how rhythm in a line can re-create actions such as digging or ploughing
- **rhyme** – emphasising words, or making you aware of the way the poem is organised
- **word patterns** – which emphasise or link words together
- **organisation** – for example, how verse structure is used to mark changes or create a flow of ideas.

You need to have:

- a clear idea of what each term means (see *Glossary* page 95)
- found some good examples from each poem to talk about.

You can mark the examples in your copy of the *Anthology* ready for use in the examination.

Sample questions

Foundation Tier

1   What does Heaney show about his relationship with his father in 'Digging' and 'Follower' and how does he present the relationship?

2   How do Heaney's words show what country life is like? You should consider how he describes the following:
- how things feel
- how things smell
- what things look like
- the sounds he describes.

3   Heaney writes about his past in a number of poems. Write about two poems in which he does this. You could comment on:
- the places, people, and events he remembers
- how Heaney reacts to them
- what Heaney was like as a child and how he changed
- the language he uses.

Higher Tier

1   In 'Digging' and 'Follower' Heaney is thinking about his father. How do these two poems give you different ideas about his relationship with his father?

2   How does Heaney use words to capture early sensations, such as sound, smell, touch and sight? Refer to 'The Early Purges' and at least one other poem in your answer.

3   How does Heaney treat the experience of moving from childhood to adulthood in his poetry? Refer to 'Mid-Term Break' and at least one other poem in your answer.

Looking at the detail

1   Look at the behaviour of the peasants, the father and the mother:
    a) what does the poet tell you about each of them?
    b) what impression does the poet create of their behaviour?
2   Make a picture of each of these images in your mind, then decide how the poet feels about what he is describing:
    a) 'The peasants came like swarms of flies and buzzed the name of God a hundred times to paralyse the Evil One.' (lines 8–10)
    b) 'throwing giant scorpion shadows' (line 12)
    c) '... they sat around ...
        the peace of understanding on each face.' (lines 29–31)
    d) 'My father, sceptic, rationalist, trying every curse and blessing' (lines 36–7)
    e) 'I watched the flame feeding on my mother' (line 41)
    f) 'I watched the holy man perform his rites' (line 42)
3   How does the poet suggest his mother got better?

Thinking about a different culture

How do Nissim Ezekiel's home, his neighbours and the whole experience of his mother being ill differ from what might happen in this country? Make a list of all the differences you can find.

For background information on Nissim Ezekiel's life, see page 89.

Writing

Imaginative

1   It's great when your friends or neighbours come round to help you or your family when you have a problem ... or is it? Write a short story or poem about just such an event.
2   Write a story which ends with the words 'my mother only said ...'

About the poem

1   What does the poem show you about the local customs of Ezekiel's native India?
2   How does Ezekiel use the description of local customs to emphasise the danger his mother is in, and how he felt about it as a child? You may like to look at:
    a) what the peasants do and say
    b) their attitude to his mother's suffering
    c) how Ezekiel describes them and the atmosphere he creates
    d) the response of his mother and father to their help.

Poem at Thirty-Nine

How I miss my father
I wish he had not been
so tired
when I was
5   born.

Writing deposit slips and checks
I think of him.
He taught me how.
This is the form,
10   he must have said:
the way it is done.
I learned to see
bits of paper
as a way
15   to escape
the life he knew
and even in high school
had a savings
account.

20   He taught me
that telling the truth
did not always mean
a beating;
though many of my truths

25   must have grieved him
before the end.

How I miss my father!
He cooked like a person
dancing
30   in a yoga meditation
and craved the voluptuous
sharing
of good food.

Now I look and cook just like him:
35   my brain light;
tossing this and that
into the pot;
seasoning none of my life
the same way twice; happy to feed
40   whoever strays my way.

He would have grown
to admire
the woman I've become:
cooking, writing, chopping wood,
45   staring into the fire.

Alice Walker

Explanations

deposit slips: pieces of paper showing the amount of money paid into a bank account
checks: the American spelling of 'cheques'
craved: longed for
voluptuous: appealing to the senses of touch, taste, smell, sight and hearing

First impressions

1 What habits has Alice Walker learnt from her father?

2 How does she feel about her relationship with her father?

3 Which words or phrases did you find most striking as you read the poem?

4 How would you describe Walker's father after reading the poem?

A closer look

5 How does the poet's mood change during the poem and how does she signal the change?

6 What hopes did Walker's father have for his daughter?

7 Look closely at lines 28–33. What does Walker reveal about her father here?

8 How does the way the poem is organised create a sense of Walker growing up?

9 What feelings does the poet have towards the woman she has become?

Looking at the language

Explain what Walker is trying to communicate through these descriptions:

a) '... many of my truths must have grieved him before the end' (lines 24–26)

b) 'my brain light' (line 35)

c) 'seasoning none of my life the same way twice' (lines 38–39).

Writing

Imaginative

1 How do you see yourself at thirty-nine? Where will you be? What will you be doing? How will the world you live in have changed by then?

   Write a short story, description or a poem reflecting on what changes you think you will have experienced.

2 Write a poem in which each verse gives a 'snapshot' of a memory of you growing up and changing.

About the poem

How does Alice Walker's poem show that while she admired her father she also has regrets about her relationship with him?

You should think about:

● what she learnt from him
● how she describes him
● anything she wishes had been different
● her final thoughts.

Looking at both poems

In a group review the two poems, 'Night of the Scorpion' and 'Poem at Thirty-Nine', and compare what each poem has to say about:

● family life
● learning from parent(s)
● a different culture.

Which poem did you find most effective and why?

Present your findings to the rest of the class.

For background information on Alice Walker's life, see page 91.

5 Nature red

Vultures

In the greyness
and drizzle of one despondent
dawn unstirred by harbingers
of sunbreak a vulture
5   perching high on broken
bone of a dead tree
nestled close to his
mate his smooth
bashed-in head, a pebble
10 on a stem rooted in
a dump of gross
feathers, inclined affectionately
to hers. Yesterday they picked
the eyes of a swollen
15 corpse in a water-logged
trench and ate the
things in its bowel. Full
gorged they chose their roost
keeping the hollowed remnant
20 in easy range of cold
telescopic eyes ...
     Strange
indeed how love in other
ways so particular
25 will pick a corner
in that charnel-house
tidy it and coil up there, perhaps
even fall asleep – her face
turned to the wall!

30 ... Thus the Commandant at Belsen
Camp going home for
the day with fumes of
human roast clinging
rebelliously to his hairy
35 nostrils will stop
at the wayside sweet-shop
and pick up a chocolate
for his tender offspring
waiting at home for Daddy's
40 return ...
     Praise bounteous
providence if you will
that grants even an ogre
a tiny glow-worm
45 tenderness encapsulated
in icy caverns of a cruel
heart or else despair
for in the very germ
of that kindred love is
50 lodged the perpetuity
of evil.

Chinua Achebe

*E*xplanations

harbingers: heralds announcing that someone or something is about to arrive
charnel-house: place (often below ground) where the bodies of the dead are placed
Belsen Camp: a concentration camp in which Jewish and other prisoners were held and killed by the Nazis during the Second World War
bounteous providence: all good things that God gives to humanity
encapsulated in: wrapped up inside
is lodged the perpetuity of evil: evil is fixed forever

Note

The last section (lines 41–51) consists of one complicated sentence. What the poet is saying is that you can choose to:
- praise God that even the most wicked creature has a spark of good, or
- despair because that spark of good has evil fixed to it for ever.

The broad picture

1 The first section (lines 1–21) describes two vultures. What do we see them doing?
2 What did they do 'yesterday'?
3 In lines 22–29 the poet tells us his thoughts and feelings about what he has seen. What are they?
4 He compares the vultures to a concentration camp commandant (lines 30–40). Why?
5 The end of the poem (lines 41–51) offers us a choice of how we can think about love and evil. Which side do you agree with?

Looking at the detail

6 What is the atmosphere at the beginning of the poem and how is it created? (lines 1–4)
7 Look at these phrases from lines 5–12: '... broken bone ...', 'bashed-in head ...' 'dump of gross feathers ...'

Why did the poet choose these words and how do they contribute to the overall effect?
8 Comment in a similar way on the choice of language in lines 13–17.
9 How does the writer describe love in lines 22–29? What is the effect of the word 'her' (line 28)?
10 Why do you think the writer uses the words 'roast' and 'rebelliously' (lines 33 and 34)? What do they suggest to you?
11 The final section (lines 41–51) contains two pairs of contrasting images. What are they and how effective do you find them?

For information about Chinua Achebe's life, see page 88.

Writing about the poem

Write an account of what the poem says and your response to it. You should write at least four paragraphs, describing:
- what the poet sees (lines 1–21)
- what he thinks about it (lines 22–40)
- what he says we can learn from it about life (lines 41–51)
- your own thoughts and feelings about what he says.

Sacrifice

As he moves the knife across the neck of the goat
I can feel its point on my throat;
And as the blood geysers from the jugular,
A hot and sticky sweat breaks out on my body.

5   We are laying the foundations of a friend's house.
After a brief prayer that all who dwell here
May be blessed, we stand in a tight circle
Around the animal to be sacrificed; it has
A civilized and patient look. The glare of the sun,
10   The heat, and the smell of blood make me dizzy.

The knife is with my friend; it is a necessary
Part of the ritual that it is his hand only
Which should draw the blood. How keenly it cuts!
The movement is a little unsteady, perhaps,
15   But forgive him, this is his first butchering.
Four calloused hands imprison my jerking legs.

The children are fascinated by the tableau,
And watch in satisfaction the blood flow
Into the hastily dug hole. Two spadefuls of dirt
20   Will cover me up for ever. A white-bearded man
Chants something holy, and feebly thrusts the pick
Into the virgin ground; the cameras click.

We are not laying the foundations of a house,
But another Dachau.

Taufiq Rafat

Explanations

geysers: gushes as if from an underground spring
jugular: the main vein in the neck
calloused: rough and hardened by work
tableau: living picture
Dachau: a concentration camp in which Jewish and other prisoners were held and killed by the Nazis during the Second World War

The broad picture

1 The poem describes a sacrifice. What is the purpose of this sacrifice?
2 Who is performing it and why?
3 Who else is present?
4 How does the writer feel at the moment the goat is killed?
5 In the last two lines he sums up his feelings about the whole ceremony. What does he mean?

How the story is told

6 The poem is like a newspaper report; it does not present the events in the order in which they happened. To do that, you would need to read it in this order:
   a) lines 5–13
   'We are laying ... draw the blood'
   b) lines 1–4
   'As he moves ... on my body'
   c) lines 10–24
   'How keenly it cuts! ... another Dachau.'
Try reading the poem in that order. How does it alter the poem's impact? Why did the poet choose the order he did?

7 Although the story is told by one person, we get several different points of view. What do we learn about the thoughts and feelings of each of the following?
   ● the narrator
   ● the children
   ● the other onlookers
   ● the goat.
8 The writer speaks with two voices:
   a) as himself
   b) as himself imagining that he is the goat.
   In which sections of the poem does he do each of these? What is the effect of these shifts?

For information on Taufiq Rafat's life, see page 90.

Writing about the poem

1 The ceremony that this poem describes comes from a culture that is different from the one that is traditional in Britain. What does the poem tell us about:
   ● the culture of that society?
   ● the poet's own thoughts and feelings about it?
2 Would you say that the poet sees himself as an outsider or an insider in the ceremony he is describing? Write about the poem from this point of view.

A Cautionary Tale

... we had sold our death ... for the sum of £70.18s.6d. and lent our fear ... on interest of £3.10s.0d. per month, so we did not care about death and we did not fear again.

From *The Palm Wine Drinkard* by Amos Tutuola

She met a lion face to face
As she went walking
Up to her hips in grass
On the wild savannah.
5   So close they stood they touched
If she put out her thumb
Or he his soft ferocious paw.
She bore no weight of fear,
For only yesterday
10   She'd leased it to a rich man, poor
In that commodity.
Without her terror she was free
From the alarming smell
That irritates a lion
15   And makes him lash his tail.
And so he yawned, and stretched
On the long stemmed grasses,
And in the pouring sun
She sat beside his royalty
20   And sang to him a tale of moon.
Before he rose to go
He opened wide his jaw
And took between his teeth
Her wishing bone, as if to say,
25   I could, you know.
A rich man had her caution
So she laughed; cool,
In the lion's ear, her pretty breath.
What happened next happens
30   To every maiden fair
Who lends her fear
But forgets to sell her death:
The lion ate her up, and down
To the smallest crumb.
35   Lord have mercy upon
Her sweet white bones. Amen.

Anne Wilkinson

Thinking about the poem

1 The poem is like a fairy story. What parts of it suggest this?
2 It is called 'A Cautionary Tale'. Is this a good title? What are the reasons for your opinion?
3 Is this poem anything more than an entertaining and light-hearted story?

For information on Anne Wilkinson's life, see page 91.

Explanations

Cautionary Tale: entertaining story for children with a moral. It warned children that if they behaved badly, in a particular way, terrible things might happen to them. A famous one tells of the terrible things that happened to 'Matilda who told such dreadful lies'

£70.18s.6d./£3.10s.0d.: pre-decimal currency. 's' = shillings, 'd' = pence. The amounts are £70–92.5 and £3.50

Writing

Imaginative

What would it be like to 'lend your fear' and live without any kind of fear at all? The poem describes one of the drawbacks. Think of another emotion that you might get rid of by lending it to someone else. For example:

● anger
● hatred
● worry.

There would be great advantages – as the girl in the poem discovered. Would there be any drawbacks?
Write a story about the person who lent their _____, but forgot to sell their _____.

Looking at all three poems

Thinking about animals

1 People who write about animals sometimes describe them as if they were human and could have the same thoughts and feelings as us. This is called 'anthropomorphism'. Are any of these poems written in this way?

2 Writers often make animals the centre of a poem or story not because of what they are but because they lead on to thoughts about other, more important things. Do any of these poems do this?

3 Two of the poems refer to Nazi concentration camps in which millions of Jewish people were gassed, poisoned or starved to death. But they are about vultures and a goat. Is this connection too far-fetched, or have the writers something important to say?

Thinking about different cultures

4 All three poems in this section were written by poets with a particular background of ideas and a particular upbringing. What do we learn about their cultures from reading these poems?

5 Do any of them have comments to make about the society in which they live?

6 What do you learn from any of the poems about life in a different culture?

Writing

Imaginative

1 Write a conversation between an animal rights activist and someone who thinks animals are there to be used by human beings. They both express their ideas forcibly and clearly. How does the conversation end?

2 Imagine that you have come to Britain from a different country and find much that goes on here very different. Choose an everyday 'ritual' and write a description of it as an outsider.

About the poems

3 Look back over your responses to the questions in *Thinking about animals* and write about how any two of the poets use animals in their poems.

4 Look back over your responses to the questions in *Thinking about different cultures* and write about how any one of the poems reveals the background and ideas of the poet.

Lazy Man's Song

I could have a job, but I am too lazy to choose it;
I have got land, but am too lazy to farm it.
My house leaks; I am too lazy to mend it.
My clothes are torn; I am too lazy to darn them.
5   I have got wine, but I am too lazy to drink;
So it's just the same as if my cup were empty.
I have got a lute, but I am too lazy to play;
So it's just the same as if it had no strings.
My family tells me there is no more steamed rice;
10   I want to cook, but I am too lazy to grind.
My friends and relatives write me long letters;
I should like to read them, but they're such a bother to open.
I have always been told that Hsi Shuh-yeh
Passed his whole life in absolute idleness.
15   But he played his lute and sometimes worked at his forge;
So even he was not so lazy as I.

Po Chü-I

Explanations

lute: a stringed instrument
    similar to a guitar
forge: a blacksmith's
    workshop

First impressions

Imagine you are this man's child and he is now dead. Write his obituary explaining what he was like, especially as a father.

For a description of the life of Po Chü-I, see page 90.

Looking at the language

1 Why is the poem described as a 'Song'?
2 Which words or phrases struck you most vividly while reading the poem?

Looking at the detail

3 How poor is this man?
4 Pick out words or phrases which you think best reveal his attitude to his lifestyle.
5 Do you agree with what the man says in lines 6 and 8?
6 Which lines would you use to prove this man treats other people badly?
7 How does the poet's organisation and use of language create the idea of laziness?
8 What do you think the poet expects the reader to feel towards this man? Give reasons for your answer.
9 Is there any evidence that this poem is not meant to be taken entirely seriously?

Laziness

Which of the following statements best describes the poem? Give reasons for your choice.
a) The man in the poem benefits from being lazy.
b) Po Chü-I shows laziness can be a good quality.
c) The poem shows that laziness is always bad and it leads to unhappiness.

Different cultures

Which details make it clear that this poem is Chinese?

Writing

Imaginative

Write a modern-day version of this poem choosing a different type of person to write about. Make sure every detail you include fits in with your individual's lifestyle.

About the poem

How effectively does this poem portray the lifestyle and attitude of the man in its title? You could think about:
a) how his lifestyle is described
b) the way he speaks
c) the way in which the poem is written.

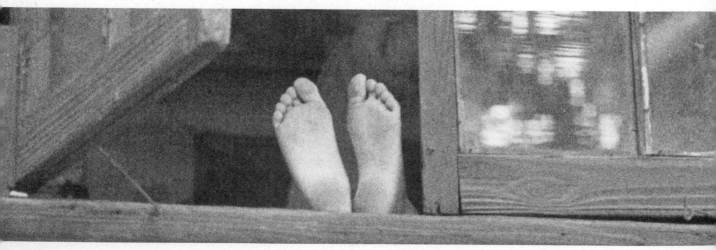

Poverty Poems – 2

I lifted up my eyes
near the railway station
and saw a leper standing
against a poster-ridden wall.

5   Silent, a beggar,
he did not beg.
Offered a coin
he took it
without a glance at me
10 nor made the slightest gesture
in acknowledgement. Perhaps
he was dumb and deaf as well.

Dumb and deaf
I walk along
15 leper-image sinking in my eyes.
There was another on the platform:
he sang with zest in praise of God
like a happy saint
which perhaps he was ...
20 I walk along,
leper-music holding up my mind.

Nissim Ezekiel

Explanations

leper: a person with
   leprosy, an infectious,
   and deforming, skin
   disease
zest: enthusiasm

First impressions

What would you include in a charity poster based on this poem?

Looking at the language

1 How does Nissim Ezekiel picture himself at the start of the poem?
2 What does the poet notice about each leper?
3 Which words or phrases did you find most effective?
4 How does the poet feel about each of the lepers?

Looking at the detail

5 What does the first line suggest the poet had been doing before?
6 What surprises him in lines 5–6?
7 Explain in your own words the meaning and the impact of the phrases: 'poster-ridden', 'dumb and deaf', 'leper-image' and 'leper-music'.
8 Do you agree with the reasons the poet gives for:
   a) the first leper's silence
   b) the second leper's singing?
   Do you think the poet is convinced by what he says?
9 How does the poet show that each beggar has affected him?
10 Explain what 'holding up' means in the last line.

Different cultures

Which words, phrases or ideas make you most aware that this poem is set in India?

Looking at both poems

1 Decide whether you agree with each statement and explain your answer.
   a) Both poems make it clear how awful being poor is.
   b) Neither poet seems to understand poor people.
   c) The poems suggest that poor people do not help themselves.
   d) Although the poems come from different cultures they are still relevant to us.
2 Make a chart showing the similarities and differences between the two poems.
3 Giving reasons, explain which poem you find most effective.

For information on Nissim Ezekiel's life, see page 89.

Writing

Imaginative

1 Sometimes we may see a person for just a short period of time but they can still make a strong impression on us. Write about meeting or seeing someone briefly and how this changed the way you thought or felt. Make sure you:
   - explain what was special about the person
   - why you were affected
   - what difference it made to you.
2 Write a story or a poem about two of your friends who know each other, but who are very different people. Start by considering what it is about each that you like and dislike, and how well they get on together.

Slave time

Mama Dot

Born on a sunday
in the kingdom of Ashante

Sold on monday
into slavery

5 Ran away on tuesday
cause she born free

Lost a foot on wednesday
when they catch she

Worked all thursday
10 till her head grey

Dropped on friday
where they burned she

Freed on saturday
in a new century   *Fred D'Aguiar*

Looking at the whole poem

1 This poem tells a story. What are the main events of the story?
2 What is the pattern of the poem?
3 What feelings about slavery does the poem express?

Looking at the language

This poem is based on a common nursery rhyme idea. You may have heard rhymes like 'The tale of Solomon Grundy' which follow a similar pattern.

4 The subject of the poem is a serious one. Why do you think the writer chose this 'childish' form?
5 At certain points the writer uses language that is not standard English.
    ● What are they?
    ● Why does he do this?

Explanations

Ashante: (sometimes spelled 'Ashanti'), a kingdom in West Africa in the time of the slave trade; part of what is now Ghana

a new century: slavery was officially abolished in western Europe and the United States of America during the nineteenth century, so her 'new century' can be both her life after death and the life of freed slaves after abolition.

Writing

The central character in Fred D'Aguiar's poem represents all slaves, rather than being a particular person. Choose a similar central character; for example:
● the politician
● the television star
● the homeless person.
Write the story of their life following a similar simple pattern.

Limbo

And limbo stick is the silence in front of me
limbo

limbo
limbo like me
5   *limbo*
limbo like me

long dark night is the silence in front of me
limbo
limbo like me

10   stick hit sound
and the ship like it ready

stick hit sound
and the dark still steady

limbo
15   *limbo like me*

long dark deck and the water surrounding me
long dark deck and the silence is over me

limbo
limbo like me

20   stick is the whip
and the dark deck is slavery

stick is the whip
and the dark deck is slavery

limbo
25   *limbo like me*

drum stick knock
and the darkness is over me

knees spread wide
and the water is hiding

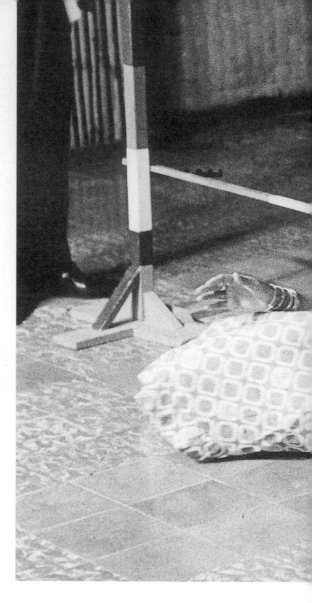

30   *limbo*
limbo like me

knees spread wide
and the dark ground is under me

down
35   down
down

and the drummer is calling me

limbo
limbo like me

40   sun coming up
and the drummers are praising me

out of the dark
and the dumb gods are raising me

up
45 up
up

and the music is saving me

hot
slow
50 step

on the burning ground.

Edward Kamau Brathwaite

Explanations

limbo: in the Caribbean, limbo means a dance in which the person dancing has to lean further and further backwards to pass beneath a stick which is held parallel to the ground. The most skilful dancers can dance under a pole only a few inches off the ground. In order to do this, as the poem describes, the dancer must spread his knees wide to lower his body and keep his balance as he leans backward. Then, as he passes underneath the pole, he can gradually raise his body again, always keeping time to the rhythm of the music.

The word limbo also has a completely different meaning. Some Christian tradition holds that it is the dark and dismal place where unbaptised babies go when they die; because they have not entered the church they cannot go to heaven. It is also used to mean any unpleasant place where things or people are put when people want to get rid of them

Looking at the whole poem

As the title tells us, this poem is about a limbo dancer.

1 Which lines describe the dance being done?

2 The poem is also about something else. What do the following phrases tell you about that 'something else'?
- 'long dark night'
- 'the ship'
- 'the whip'
- 'the water surrounding me'.

3 There is one line, repeated, which tells you the main subject of the poem. Which one is it?

4 The poem tells the story of the limbo dance. It also tells the story of people being taken into slavery and the two stories run parallel for much of the way. But what happens in the end? Look especially at lines 28–33 and 40–43.

Dramatic reading

Someone who has never seen a limbo dance may find it difficult to imagine, but the poet makes it much easier, not only by the way he describes it but also by the rhythm of the verse. Work out a group reading of the poem that makes that rhythm clear.

5 Discuss the effect you want to achieve.

6 Decide how the poem should be arranged. Lines can be spoken by one or more voices. You could also try repeating parts of the poem as a background rhythm for other parts.

7 Decide who will read which parts.

8 Try out your reading.

9 Continue practising and discussing it until you are satisfied.

Writing about both poems

1 The two poets each give us a picture of their people's history. Write about the two poems describing:
- the history each tells us
- how the poem tells its story
- the impact each has on the reader.

You should finish by commenting on how effective you think each one is and which one you prefer, if you have a preference.

2 Both poems describe slavery from an angle:
- Fred D'Aguiar uses a nursery rhyme format
- E. K. Brathwaite uses the image of the limbo dancer.

Write a comparison of the two poems in which you not only explain what each is saying but also describe the method each uses. Finish by assessing the effectiveness of the two approaches.

For information on Edward Kamau Brathwaite's life, see page 88.

Wha Fe Call I'

Miss Ivy, tell mi supmn,
An mi wan' yuh ansa good.
When yuh eat roun 12 o'clock,
Wassit yuh call yuh food?

5   For fram mi come yah mi confuse,
An mi noh know which is right,
Weddah dinnah a de food yuh eat midday,
Or de one yuh eat a night.

Mi know sey breakfus a de mawnin one,
10   But cyan tell ef suppa a six or t'ree,
An one ting mi wi nebba undastan,
Is when yuh hab yuh tea.

Miss A dung a London ha lunch 12 o'clock,
An dinnah she hab bout t'ree,
15   Suppah she hab bout six o'clock,
But she noh hab noh tea.

Den mi go a Cambridge todda day,
Wi hab dinnah roun' bout two,
T'ree hour later mi frien she sey,
20   Mi hungry, how bout yuh?

Joe sey im tink a suppa time,
An mi sey yes, mi agree,
She halla, 'Suppa? a five o'clock,
Missus yuh mussa mean tea!'

25   Den Sunday mi employer get up late,
Soh she noh hab breakfus nor lunch,
But mi hear she a talk bout 'Elevenses'
An one sinting dem call 'Brunch'.

Breakfus, elevenses, an brunch,
30   lunch, dinnah, suppa, tea,
Mi brain cyan wuk out which is which,
An when a de time fe hab i'.

For jus' when mi mek headway,
Sinting dreadful set mi back,
35   And dis when mi tink mi know them all,
Mi hear bout one name snack.

Mi noh tink mi a badda wid no name,
Mi dis a nyam when time mi hungry,
For doah mi 'tomach wi glad fe de food,
40   I' couldn care less whey mi call i'.

Valerie Bloom

Explanations

Wha Fe Call I': what do you call it
supmn: something
ansa: answer
roun: around
Wassit: what is it
For fram mi come yah mi confuse: for from my coming here I have been confused
Weddah: whether
mawnin: morning
cyan: can't
nebba: never
dung: down
todda: the other
halla: holler or shout
mussa: must
sinting: something
An when a de time fe hab i': and when is the time to have it
Mi noh tink mi a badda: I don't think I'll bother
Mi dis a nyam: I devour
doah: though
wi glad: will be happy

What does it mean?

The poem is written in a form of English called *patois*. If you find this form of English hard to understand, work through the poem, making a list of words or lines that confuse you. Use the poem 'Explanations' to help you work out meanings.

You will also find it helpful to actually to say the lines to yourself. If you are doing this work as a group, try reading the poem aloud to each other to help your understanding. Once you feel you have a good idea of what the poem is saying, try producing a version of it in your own dialect.

Describing the poem

Discuss these four descriptions of Valerie Bloom's poem. Try to agree which one gives the best sense of what the poem is doing.

a) The poem shows how confusing language is when people do not use it in the same way.

b) The poem enjoys exploring the local variations you find in language use.

c) The poem is making fun of people who try to impress other people.

d) The poem is about people's desire to label things in a way that they think is correct. It is having fun at their expense.

Meal guide

Valerie Bloom makes fun in her poem of the confusions created by what people call their meals.

Make an alphabetical guide to meals based on what Valerie Bloom discovered. Your guide should cover when different people eat particular meals. You can also include your own experience of mealtimes and their names.

For information on Valerie Bloom's life, see page 88.

Writing

Imaginative

1   Write a conversation based on your own mealtime experiences. It could be:
   ● your family at breakfast, lunch or dinner
   ● with your friends in the school canteen
   ● out somewhere
   ● at a friend's house.

2   Write a monologue in which a character talks about some aspect of food. Try to include a sense of confusion, complaint and humour in the same way that Valerie Bloom does. Here are some possible starting points:
   ● foods that some people refuse to eat
   ● the way people cook food
   ● the way people eat their food
   ● food in restaurants and cafes.

About the poem

3   Write about the thoughts and feelings that Valerie Bloom expresses in her poem. Do you think there is a serious point behind the humour or is it simply a piece of fun?

Study No. X

chi ama, crede : mother

well

told me

unmaternally

5   for there was no sex involved (just

a

cosmos

of love) rare

in these times & spaces made of cracked-nut hearts; &

10   split

pea

skulls;

infanta! madonna! guernica! hiroshima!

)you are a catastrophe on the mirror of this earth

15   )you do not

let me

believe

(in hell

only: & it takes more courage

20   than red

wheelbarrows

give

to love:

flesh & dust

Pierre Coupey

Explanations

No.: abbreviation for 'number'

chi ama, crede: an Italian phrase meaning 'who loves, believes'. In English, we might say, 'the person who loves also believes'

unmaternally: in a way that is not like a mother

cosmos: universe

infanta: daughter of the King of Spain

madonna: the Virgin Mary

guernica: a town in Spain which was bombed during the Spanish Civil War, the first time civilians had ever been attacked in this way. Picasso made a famous painting about it.

hiroshima: a city in Japan where one of the first nuclear bombs was dropped

catastrophe: major disaster

red wheelbarrows: William Carlos Williams wrote a poem called 'The Red Wheelbarrow'. That poem can be interpreted in many ways, which is one of the points of this poem: it is about the way people see objects, about what you can see in a scene

flesh & dust: the Bible says that humans come from the dust of the earth at the start of the world and return to dust at the end of their life. The phrase can be seen as a reference to our lives

Parts of the puzzle

● What might the poem mean?
● Does it mean anything at all?

One way to start making up your mind is to concentrate on what you do understand. Write down anything you think the poem might be saying.

These seven questions will help you. You may not find an answer for all of them. After you have attempted them, try to think of other questions of your own which you can answer as well.

1 What does the poem say about belief? (line 1)

2 What might be the poet's mother's attitude to love and sex? (lines 1–8)

3 What is the world like today in terms of love and sex? (lines 8–12)

4 What might connect or explain the four things in line 13: 'infanta! madonna! guernica! hiroshima!'

5 Who might be 'you' in lines 14 and 15?

6 What do you find out about the poet's beliefs? (lines 15–19)

7 What might the title mean?

Views of the poem

There is often no single answer to the question of what a poem means.

Look at these four views. Use them as starting points for a discussion of the poem or to start your own thinking. Can you find evidence that supports or contradicts any of these views?

● The poem is mainly about the poet's inability to rid himself of the beliefs that he has been taught, however much he questions and doubts.

● The poem is about gathering the courage to love someone in spite of the dangers involved.

● The poem is about becoming involved: something his mother never did.

● The two verses are different aspects of his life. The first is the world he has grown up in. The second is his attempt to be more than just an observer.

Looking at the form

The poem has:
- no rhyme scheme
- no regular rhythm
- no regular line length
- unconventional use of punctuation
- many very short lines
- two parts.

Poets are often concerned with how a poem looks on the page as well as its meaning.

The poet appears to have deliberately created a sense of words having been scattered everywhere. As you look at this poem, think why the writer might have chosen to present it in this way.

1   Look at the punctuation in the poem.
    - What punctuation is used and what punctuation is left out?
    - Why do you think the poet has chosen to use punctuation in this way?
      Think about the effect it has on you.
2   Look at the shape of the poem.
    - Does the poet use sentences?
    - How has the poet used shape and positioned his words?
      Think about the effect this has on you.
3   Why do you think the poet has used foreign words in this poem?
4   Does the presentation of the poem help to put across what the poem is about? You might like to consider what the poem says about love, death and war.

For information on Pierre Coupey's life, see page 89.

Writing

Imaginative

1   Write a poem or a short piece of prose about the uncertainties you face now and in the near future. You could write about:
    - school
    - exams
    - home
    - jobs
    - relationships.

About the poem

2   A friend has come to you and said he does not understand the poem at all and is in a panic in case it comes up in the examination. Write down in a simple and straightforward way for your friend what you have found out about the poem. You could include comments on:
    - the form of the poem
    - possible meanings
    - parts which are difficult but about which you now have some thoughts
    - the poem's overall effect.

For Forest

Forest could keep secrets
Forest could keep secrets

Forest tune in everyday
to watersound and birdsound
5   Forest letting her hair down
to the teeming creeping of her forest-ground

But Forest don't broadcast her business
no Forest cover her business down
from sky and fast-eye sun
10   and when night come
and darkness wrap her like a gown
Forest is a bad dream woman

Forest dreaming about mountain
and when earth was young
15   Forest dreaming of the caress of gold
Forest rootsing with mysterious eldorado

and when howler monkey
wake her up with howl
Forest just stretch and stir
20   to a new day of sound

but coming back to secrets
Forest could keep secrets
Forest could keep secrets
   And we must keep Forest

Grace Nichols

Explanations

teeming: bursting, buzzing, swarming
her business: what she does
caress: touch, embrace, hug
rootsing: living to its very core
eldorado: precious magic, amazing opportunity – Eldorado was originally the name of a legendary city that was supposed to have riches beyond an explorer's wildest dreams
howler monkey: a monkey that is known for its strange cry – hence its name

Feelings about the forest

Grace Nichols was clearly impressed by her visit to the forests of Guyana. For a description of her visit, see page 90. Choose three of these words which best describe her impression of the forest:

- exciting
- frightening
- puzzling
- mysterious
- unfathomable
- dreamy
- enjoyable
- secretive
- elusive

The way the poem is written

In Grace Nichols' poem the forest is treated as if it were a person. The literary term for this is personification. More important than knowing the word is sensing the effect that this has in making the poem work.

1 Make a list of all the things that the forest does and is. These are the first two:
- keeps secrets
- tunes in to the sounds of water and birds calling.

2 Look at the list you have made.
- Explain any phrases that you think puzzle those who read the poem.
- Describe the kind of woman that the forest is.

3 Look at words and phrases that are repeated. What do these repetitions highlight?

The picture of the forest

What does each of the verses in the poem bring to mind or make you think about the forest?

Try to think about both the meaning of the words and the effect of the imagery on you individually. This is how one person started:

'**Verse 1:** The forest is a very private place which it is difficult to find out about (or even travel in)

Verse 2: The forest has background sounds, just like you sometimes have a radio on in the background. I see her as a tall ...'

Writing

Descriptive / imaginative

1   Write about a journey of your own to somewhere very different from the place where you live. This does not have to be to somewhere exotic and strange, just different. It could be based on:

- a day trip
- a holiday
- staying with relatives or friends
- moving house
- a student exchange.

You should try to base it on an actual journey but you can use your imagination if you cannot remember such a journey.

2   Grace Nichols' poem is called 'For Forest'. Write your own poem in which a place is brought to life in the same way. Here are some possibilities:

- For City
- For River
- For Hospital
- For Farm
- For House.

Alternatively you could use the name of the area where you live.

About the poem

3   Write about the way that Grace Nichols has brought the forest to life in her poem. You could include:

- your thoughts about the overall impression (look back at 'Feelings about the forest')
- your thoughts about the way the forest is seen as a person (look back at 'The way the poem is written')
- your thoughts about the way the impression develops verse by verse (look back at 'The picture of the forest')
- any final thoughts, especially about the meaning of the last line.

For information on Grace Nichols' life, see page 90.

Selected books by Grace Nichols

I is a Long Memoried Woman, Karnak Ilo, 1990
The Fat Black Woman's Poems, Virago, 1984
Lazy Thoughts of a Lazy Woman, Virago, 1989
Whole of a Morning Sky (novel), Virago, 1986
Give Yourself a Hug (children's poetry), Black, 1994

Poems from other cultures and traditions: exam practice

Foundation Tier

1 Choose **two** poems in which a member of a family is described. Explain how the poet has used words and details to:
   - describe that person
   - create the atmosphere of the home
   - show what family life is like in their culture.

   Explain which poem you prefer giving reasons for your choice. Poems to choose from:

   - **'Vultures'**
   - **'Lazy Man's Song'**
   - **'Night of the Scorpion'**
   - **'Poem at Thirty-Nine'.**

2 Write about what you have found out about the beliefs and customs of other cultures from **two** of the following poems. Explain how the poet has used language to make them vivid and interesting. Poems to choose from:

   - **'Poverty Poems – 2'**
   - **'Night of the Scorpion'**
   - **'Sacrifice'**
   - **'Poem at Thirty-Nine'**
   - **'Study No. X'.**

3 Several of the poems in this section reveal a sense of fear or concern. Write about **two** poems which you feel have communicated those kinds of feelings. You could choose:

   - **'Night of the Scorpion'**
   - **'For Forest'**
   - **'Sacrifice'.**

4 What would you lose and/or gain if you swapped your world for the worlds described in **two** of the poems from other cultures and traditions? You could choose:

   - **'Lazy Man's Song'**
   - **'Poverty Poems – 2'**
   - **'For Forest'**
   - **'Sacrifice'**
   - **'Poem at Thirty-Nine'.**

5   Several of the poems in this collection tell a story. Choose **two** of them to write about. You might:
- Re-tell the story of the poem.
- Comment on how the poet tells the story.
- Explain carefully why the poet tells that story.
- Comment on the effect the poem had on you.

You could choose from:

- **'Mama Dot'**
- **'Limbo'**
- **'Vultures'**
- **'A Cautionary Tale'**
- **'Sacrifice'**
- **'Night of the Scorpion'.**

6   Choose **two** poems from this list:

- **'Wha Fe Call I"**
- **'A Cautionary Tale'**
- **'Lazy Man's Song'.**

For your chosen poems, describe what the poem is about and explain how it uses humour to get its point across.

7   Some of the poems in this section use non-standard English. Choose **two or three** of these poems and comment on the way in which they use language. You could comment on:
- the kind of language they use
- the effect it has on the reader
- why you think the poet chose to write in this form.

Poems you could choose from are:

- **'Wha Fe Call I"**
- **'Limbo'**
- **'Mama Dot'**
- **'For Forest'.**

8   What impression did these poems from other cultures and traditions have on you? Choose **two** poems that created a particularly strong response. Explain how you reacted to them and why. You can choose poems that produced a positive or negative response, but in either case make sure that you explain clearly and fully why you responded in that way.

The poets

Chinua Achebe

Chinua Achebe was born in Nigeria in 1931 and educated in Government College, Umatua, and University College, Ibadan. He worked in the Nigerian Broadcasting Corporation in Lagos and for Voice of Nigeria before the Nigerian civil war when he was employed in the service of the Biafran Government. He has been awarded a number of fellowships at several Nigerian and American universities where he has taught.

He has also become established as a writer of novels and poetry. Major themes in his writing include prejudice and social injustice faced by Africans in the twentieth century and the lack of respect and consideration for one another, because of the evil workings of human nature.

He wrote his first novel called *Things Fall Apart* (Everyman, 1992) after becoming indignant at the way Africans were shown in European fiction. He showed that, contrary to the view of many Europeans, African society before the Europeans came was a noble and civilised one. His later novels respond to the war experiences of Nigeria and the political and social problems he encountered.

Valerie Bloom

Valerie Bloom was born and brought up in Jamaica where she trained as a teacher but actually worked as a librarian. These days she lives in England where she has taught poetry, folk music and dance. Her first poetry book was published in 1983, called *Touch Mi!, Tell Mi!* (Bogle L'Ouverture). It was followed by a book of children's verse called *Duppy Jamboree* (Cambridge University Press).

Edward Kamau Brathwaite

E. K. Brathwaite was born in Barbados 1930. He won a scholarship to study History at Cambridge University before going on to take a PhD in Jamaican History at Sussex University. From there he went to teach for several years in Ghana before returning to the Caribbean to lecture at the University of the West Indies in Jamaica.

'Limbo' is taken from a trilogy called *The Arrivants* (Oxford University Press, 1981), first published in the 1960s. Since then Brathwaite has published many books of poetry and is one of the best-known Caribbean poets. As well as writing poetry himself, he has campaigned for the recognition of Caribbean poetry throughout the world and has written about its history and traditions.

Pierre Coupey

Pierre Coupey is a French Canadian living in Canada teaching at Capilano College in Vancouver. His first book of poems called *Bring Forth the Cowards* was published in 1964 and included 'Study No. X'. He has published three further collections of his poetry since then and is working on a new one at present. His work has some of the features of 'concrete poetry' – where the shape of the poem is important, as if it were a drawing or a sculpture. Pierre is a painter as well as a poet and has shown his work in more than thirty exhibitions. He is married and has four children.

Fred D'Aguiar

Fred D'Aguiar was born in London in 1960. His parents were Guyanese and he was brought up in Guyana before coming back to London in 1972. He is a writer of poetry and fiction. His first published collection of poetry, *Mama Dot* (Chatto and Windus), is a series of poems about a larger-than-life grandmother, Mama Dot. As the poem published in this collection suggests, she is a representative of black people and their culture throughout the world. Later poems in the sequence show Mama Dot in a variety of situations and roles: as an oracle who can see into the heart of things, as a healer, provider of food, and as a commentator on the contemporary scene. Some of the poems like 'Born on a sunday' are in patois, while others are in standard English.

Nissim Ezekiel

Born in Bombay in 1924 to Israeli parents, Nissim Ezekiel grew up to become a university teacher, art critic and literary editor as well as a poet. He has lived through a very turbulent period in India's history in which the struggle for independence from British rule, the partition of Pakistan and India, and religious intolerance between Muslims, Sikhs and Hindus has led to much violence.

His writing quietly explores issues such as the collapse of faith for many people in his generation, the need to understand oneself and the world one lives in. Much of his writing is personal and autobiographical.

Ezekiel writes both in traditional verse and in free style, using a colloquial style. He makes direct statements and employs few images. The strongest influences on his poetry are British writers such as Yeats and Eliot and he relies very little on Indian traditions.

Grace Nichols

Grace Nichols was born in Guyana in 1950. After university, she worked as a journalist. She has lived in England since 1977. 'For Forest' reflects both of the countries where she has lived. It was written in England, thousands of miles away from the forest it describes. She says that the poem just came to her one morning when she was lying warmly and comfortably under the bedclothes. The memory reflected in the poem is of a visit to the forests of Guyana which Grace Nichols made many years earlier. Those forests are full of animal and plant life but relatively few people live within them. There are not many chances to visit that part of the country so the journey was just as much a mystery and an adventure for Grace Nichols as it would be for us.

Most of the forest journey was exciting and enjoyable: sailing down great rivers with the forest on either side, watching magnificent waterfalls and bathing in the small streams. One part was frightening: she spent a night on the top of a mountain during a massive thunder-storm, protected by no more than a canvas sheet for a roof.

The one thing that Grace Nichols cannot explain is why the memories of that forest came flooding back one morning years after she made the visit.

Po Chü-I

Po Chü-I was a Chinese scholar (born in AD 772, died in 846), who worked for the T'ang dynasty's government first as a censor, then as governor of several cities, before becoming Secretary of the Board of Punishments.

He wrote many poems and believed that poetry should be used to fight evil in society. Many of his poems attack the injustices of his time such as heavy taxation; the strong emphasis on military ideals; superstitions and extravagance. This made him popular with the common people but his work offended the rich and powerful and he was banished and exiled. His other poems were about his daily life with all its joys and sorrows; observations of his society; and some narrative poems.

To make sure his work could be understood by everyone, Po Chü-I chose to write in a simple and direct style, but he still managed to create powerful descriptions, argue viewpoints clearly and reveal strong emotions.

Taufiq Rafat

Taufiq Rafat was born in 1927. He has been writing poetry since the age of twelve. His poems have appeared in magazines in Australia and the United States, in English anthologies and in *First Voices*. He has also written a full-length play in English.

Alice Walker

Alice Walker's parents were descendants of freed slaves living in Georgia as share-croppers. (Share-cropping is when landowners give tenants living on their land seed to plant each season and then collect half the crop as payment). Walker was the youngest (born in 1944) and brightest of their eight children winning a scholarships to the all white Spelman College. She then went on to Sarah Lawrence College in New York.

After graduating she went back south and joined the civil rights movement working for the right to vote in Mississippi where she met Melvyn Leventhal a white, Jewish, civil rights lawyer. Their inter-racial marriage in 1967 was illegal, and the only one in Mississippi at that time. Walker began to collect folklore and histories from the poor black women she met. She used their stories in her writing. She won the Pulitzer Prize for *The Color Purple* (Women's Press) which was later turned into an Oscar-winning film by Stephen Spielberg. Now divorced with an adult daughter, she is a prolific author focusing on the themes of racism, sexism, family relationships, relationships between races and the defilement and degradation of women and the environment.

Anne Wilkinson

Anne Wilkinson was born in Toronto, Canada, in 1910, and was educated in Canada, England and the USA. She spent nearly all her life in Toronto, where she was a founding editor of a literary review. She published two volumes of poetry, *Counterpoint to Sleep* in 1951 and *The Hangman Ties the Holly* in 1955, and her *Collected Poems* were published in 1968, after her death in 1961.

Preparing for the examination

The best exam grades are achieved by people who have read the poems carefully and thought about them, and can then express their ideas in a clear and intersting way.

Reading and response

You will write best about poems that have had a strong effect on you and which you enjoy. This does not mean that you cannot write effectively about poems you don't like very much, but it is more difficult.

First reactions

1   As far as possible, try to have a positive attitude towards the poem **before** you read it. Your initial reaction is very important, but if you approach the poem in a negative way, your first reaction will be biased.

2   It is quite useful to make a few brief notes on your first thoughts and feelings about the poem to refer to later – you may well find that your later thoughts are quite different!

3   Don't be put off if your first reaction is not very positive. Poems are like people: they don't always show you their best side at first meeting and it may take time to get to know them.

Exploring

4   Don't be satisfied with your first reaction. Poems are often the result of many hours' work over a long period of time. It may need several readings before you begin to understand how a poem works and what the writer is trying to say.

5   You *can* read the poem through from beginning to end (like a story), but you should also let your mind play around with the words and ideas in the poem. Think laterally (look at the poem in new and unusual ways) and try not to reject ideas just because they may seem odd or 'mad'.

6   If possible get a copy of the poem to write on. Jot your ideas on the poem itself. As new ideas come, add them too. There is an example of how to do this on page 9.

Recording

7   However you approach the poem, keep notes of your ideas. If you spend time discussing poems in groups or in the whole class, make a note of what you and other people say. These notes will be very valuable when you come to write about the poems.

8   The instructions for the examination say this:

Remember you must bring the Anthology *with you when you sit the examination so make sure you do not lose it. It is your personal copy to work with. You may annotate the* Anthology. *Annotation means brief handwritten notes in the margin, underlinings, highlightings and symbols. You will not be allowed to take additional notes or prepared answers on loose sheets into the examination.*

When you are given your examination copy of the *Anthology*, make sure that you transfer to it useful notes you have already made.

Writing about the poems

You will probably have to write about the poems as part of your preparation for the exam. This can take up quite a lot of time, but you will learn a lot from it.

- When you write about something you have read, it forces you to sort out your ideas more fully and clearly.

- Preparing to write helps you focus on the poems and probably leads to you hearing more about other people's ideas.

- In the examination you will have to write in a similar way, so it is good practice.

Planning

You must plan what you are going to write before you begin. You can do this in your head or on paper. A few people are able to carry the outline of what they are going to say in their head. Most of us need to jot some ideas down on paper first. This process often goes through these stages.

1   **Brainstorming** – you take a couple of minutes to jot down all the ideas that come into your head.

2   **Sorting** – you arrange the ideas you have so that they make sense and will produce a piece of writing that has a beginning, a middle and an end.

3   **Quotations** – you make sure that you can quote from the poems (or sum up what they say) to back up what you are going to say.

Writing

If you have followed the advice on planning, the writing should be fairly straightforward. The most difficult thing is probably striking the right tone. Remember that when you write in an exam you are addressing someone you have never met. So you cannot be as relaxed or 'chatty' as you might be when writing something to be read by other people in your class.

It is important to make your writing as 'reader-friendly' as possible. There are several ways in which you can do this:

4   Make sure that you have your thoughts clear in your mind. It will irritate the reader if your answer wanders around and 'waffles'.

5 Begin with a strong clear opening paragraph. You don't have to answer the question in this paragraph, but it helps if you include a clear indication of:

- what your main thoughts are

- how you are going to answer the question.

6 The main body of the answer should then go through your argument clearly point by point.

7 You must support what you say with:

- quotations from the poems (placed in inverted commas: '........')

- references to what the poems say in your own words.

These references to the poems should be short and relevant. You will not get credit for writing out long extracts from the poem unless it is to illustrate the point you are making.

8 When you get to the end of your answer, write a concluding paragraph which leaves the reader in no doubt about what your answer to the question is, but try to avoid going through all the arguments all over again. If you can save one last telling point until this final paragraph (possibly with a short quotation from a poem) this will provide a very effective ending to your answer.

The exam itself

If you have prepared in the ways suggested, you should not have any great difficulty with the examination, with one possible exception. Some candidates find that they do not have enough time to do themselves justice. They either rush in and start writing straight away, without thinking first, or they take a long time to get going and then have to rush at the end or fail to finish. Some suggestions for ways of avoiding this are:

- at the beginning of the exam give yourself time to read the question paper all through and think carefully about which question(s) to tackle

- take some time to plan each answer before writing

- at the beginning of the exam work out roughly how long each section should take. You can even write down the time when you should begin and finish each section

- remember that however short the time seems – it is the same for everyone.

Good Luck!

Glossary

Words used when speaking and writing about poetry

alliteration: where two or more words begin with the same 'sound' and occur in sequence in a passage of writing or in speech,

e.g. ... *what dread grasp*
Dare its deadly terrors clasp?

assonance: where two or more similar vowel sounds within words occur in sequence in a passage of writing or in speech,

e.g. *counting bells knelling classes to a close*

ballad: a poem that tells a story; originally, ballads were written to be sung, and many still retain the simplicity and the patterns of repetition which are typical of song lyrics.

iambic metre: a pattern of an unstressed syllable followed by a stressed one: de-dum de-dum de-dum. This line by Blake is iambic:

My foe outstretched beneath the tree

See also metre, rhythm, syllable.

image: a mental picture created by the words that a writer chooses for effect. For example, in 'A Poison Tree' Blake describes his anger as if it were a tree he has planted and wants to grow.

imagery: a term which covers all the various types of image in a piece of writing.

See also image, metaphor, simile.

metaphor: a type of image which makes an implied comparison by referring to something as being the thing which it resembles,

e.g. *the trains' long cries are swallowed*
in the throats of tunnels

metre: the rhythm of the lines in a poem, created by the regular pattern of stressed and unstressed syllables.

See also iambic metre, rhythm and syllable.

narrative verse: poetry which tells a story: the commonest form of narrative verse is the ballad. Examples of narrative verse in this selection are 'A Poison Tree' (page 8), 'Mid-Term Break' (page 47), 'Mama Dot' (page 71).

narrator: the storyteller within a story or poem, who can be either the writer or the writer speaking through one or more of the characters.

onomatopoeia: the use of sounds and words that imitate the sound of what is being described

e.g. *the air stammering with gunfire*

personification: writing about ideas, abstractions or objects – for example, time, the seasons, the planets – as if they were people,

e.g. *Forest don't broadcast her business*

pun: a clever or funny play on words which look or sound similar but have different meanings.

rhyme: the repetition of similar or identical sounds at the end of, or within, lines of poetry. If a poem has a pattern of rhyming lines we can use letters to show how it works. The first line is given the letter A and so are all the lines that rhyme with it. The second letter is B and so on:

e.g.	*I was angry with my friend:*	A
	I told my wrath, my wrath did end.	A
	I was angry with my foe:	B
	I told it not, my wrath did grow.	B

rhythm: the pattern of strong and weak beats (or stresses) in poetry. **See also metre and syllable.**

setting: where and when the events of a story, play or poem take place.

simile: an image which makes a comparison by saying that one thing is like another,

e.g. *The peasants came like swarms of flies.*

sonnet: a fourteen line poem with a complicated rhyme scheme. The most common rhyme schemes are:

ABBA ABBA CDE CDE

ABAB CDCD EFEF GG

Traditionally, sonnets were written in ten syllable lines with an iambic metre.

stanza: a word meaning an individual verse in a poem, useful for making a distinction between verse (of a poem) and verse (poetry in general). Traditionally poems were written in stanzas that had a regular number of lines and a regular metre and rhyme scheme – like the poems by Blake in this anthology.

structure: the shape and organisation of a text.

style: the particular aspects of a writer's technique which produce an individual and distinctive effect.

syllable: one of the sections a word can be broken down into. These three words are shown broken down into syllables:

| 1 | 2 | 3 | | 1 | 2 | | 1 | 2 | 3 | 4 | 5 |
| qua | li | fy | | ex | pel | | un | re | mark | a | ble |

See also metre and rhythm.

symbol (symbolism): an image that is used more than once by a poet and which takes on a particular meaning and importance for that poet. Blake's poetry contains many such images.

theme: the subject or subjects covered by a writer: not simply the facts and the happenings covered in the plot, but the underlying meaning behind them. For example, the poem 'Jac Codi Baw' is about a building that has been demolished by a JCB, but its theme is the thoughtless destructiveness of human beings.

tone: the character of a piece of writing; it is determined by its intended audience and is made up of such elements as choice of vocabulary and sentence structure.

verse: an individual section of a poem; part of its formal structure. Another meaning is poetry in general. **See also stanza.**